ON BEING A REAL CHRISTIAN

by G. Christian Weiss

Back to the Bible

Lincoln, Nebraska 68501

188,000 printed to date—1987
(5-5127—5M—67)
ISBN 0-8474-0262-2

Printed in the United States of America

Foreword

When a baby comes to bless a home, the parents take precautions to protect him from disease and accident. They make every effort to give the child a properly balanced diet so that he will have a good start in life and will thus have a healthy, strong body when he is grown.

In a truly Christian home the parents will be careful to instruct the child properly in spiritual matters to fortify him for later years.

Too often, however, a newborn babe in Christ is taken for granted. Older, more mature Christians fail to see the need of protecting him from danger. They do not recognize the necessity of proper training in basic Christian doctrines and practices.

Perhaps this is one reason why Christians of this generation have been accused of lacking genuineness. However, a close study and diligent practice of the principles in this book will help young Christians avoid such a charge. It deals briefly yet adequately with many of the essential areas of Christian experience and conduct. It is exceedingly practical.

Pastors, Christian workers and evangelists will find this book invaluable in working with babes in Christ. Since the first edition was published in 1951, this book has been widely circulated in English and has been translated into a number of foreign languages for use on mission fields.

—The Publishers

Contents

Chapter 1

Salvation—God's Part

"O God—if there is a God—" Many years ago, this was how a boy of nine or ten endeavored to pray to God in a lonely spot in the woods adjacent to his home. He was experiencing a time of difficulty and desperate need. But he was not quite sure he believed in God, for he had never been taught anything about Him. However, we can see that he had an inner consciousness of the existence, somewhere, of a God who could help people.

"If You can hear me and if You will help me now, I—I—" What made him hesitate? Why couldn't this boy go on with his prayer? Though he was in desperate need of help beyond himself and though he tried to call on the God he thought could help, he suddenly realized how helpless he was to contact God. In that moment a picture of his life as he had lived it so far flashed through his mind. His sinfulness made him feel cut off from God. He sensed that he had no resources with which he could communicate with a holy God.

As the boy struggled with these thoughts, he was earnestly seeking for some way to contact the God he felt must be out there somewhere. But why

5

should God hear him and help him if He really did exist? He began to wonder if God would be pleased with some sort of bargain. So he continued his attempted prayer: "I'll read the Bible every day of my life from now on—if only You will help me."

I understand the struggle of that boy very well, for I was that boy. The experience of that dark day has lived on vividly in my memory. Actually, it proved to be a very good day for me, because God heard my boyish prayer. He helped me through the immediate difficulty, and I, in turn, kept my promise. From that day on I read the Bible daily. As I read, I discovered that it was the Word of God, that it was God's communication to the world and to me personally. What I read convicted me of my lost spiritual condition. Eventually, as I began to understand the Gospel and what Jesus Christ had done for me, I trusted Him as my personal Saviour. Needless to say, my entire life changed.

I believe my boyhood experience is similar to the experience of every person who seriously begins to consider his relationship to God or who seeks to contact God. When an unbeliever wants to turn to God in a time of need, almost immediately he is aware of his sinfulness and unworthiness. He begins to ask himself, *How can one so full of sin ever hope to talk to a holy God? How can such a sinful person have a right relationship with God?* Every human being is conscious of sin, to some extent, although some may not want to admit it openly.

This consciousness of sin is not merely the result of childhood training, nor does it come only to those

6

who read and know the Bible. Even people who have never heard of the Bible or had any religious training have that same inner consciousness of sin when they desire to approach God. Those who live in areas where they have had no exposure to the Gospel have a religion characterized by an unceasing attempt to atone for sin and to appease the displeasure of some deity. Frequently their altars are stained with the blood of animals or humans as they realize that sacrifice is necessary to atone for sin. Concerning those who are in darkness regarding the Bible and spiritual truth, the Apostle Paul wrote: "For when the Gentiles, which have not the law, do by nature the things contained in the law, these, having not the law, are a law unto themselves: which shew the work of the law written in their hearts, their conscience also bearing witness, and their thoughts the mean while accusing or else excusing one another" (Rom. 2:14,15).

You, too, may already have come face to face with your sin. You have probably become terribly conscious of the wall of sin that stands between you and God as an insurmountable barrier. Your conscience, if you are honest, tells you that you have sinned. The convicting voice of God's Spirit tells you that you have sinned. And above all, the Bible's testimony against your sin is universal, indicting and indisputable: "All have sinned, and come short of the glory of God" (Rom. 3:23). "There is none righteous, no, not one" (v. 10). "All we like sheep have gone astray; we have turned every one to his own way" (Isa. 53:6). In this group called "sinners," you

7

and I, along with all the rest of the human race, must take our place.

In addition to this consciousness of sin, we have a corresponding idea of the holiness and justice of God. We understand that God must be pure, holy, just and righteous. Therefore, He cannot tolerate sin. If He could, He would not be God, for a deity who overlooks wickedness would be no greater than a human and would cease to be God.

Even on a human level, we realize that a good judge must punish all wrongdoing. If he does not, he will soon be removed from office. A judge must pass judgment on sin. He dare not forgive or exonerate any guilty person. His position does not permit him to do so. He might have an inner desire to exonerate the guilty one in his court, but he cannot. No matter how much compassion and pity he might feel for the person, he cannot exercise it, for justice must prevail. The same is true with God and the sinful human race. He cannot ignore the guilt of our sin.

We know from the Bible that God loves people, even though they are sinful. The love of God is one of the main themes of Scripture. God loves the entire human race—every child of Adam. God loves us because He created us. Nothing else is required to merit His love. When everything else in the entire world fails you, you can still count on God's love. Even when all human love has been exhausted or withdrawn, you can still be confident that God loves you.

We cannot doubt the love of God, for the Bible is

filled with reassurances: "God so loved the world, that he gave his only begotten Son" (John 3:16). "God commendeth his love toward us, in that, while we were yet sinners, Christ died for us" (Rom. 5:8). "I have loved thee with an everlasting love" (Jer. 31:3). "When my father and my mother forsake me, then the Lord will take me up" (Ps. 27:10).

The love of God for sinners was beautifully illustrated by Christ in the parable of the Prodigal Son, found in Luke 15. Although this son had left his father and foolishly wasted his inheritance through his sinful life-style, his father still loved him and welcomed him home with tears of joy and the kiss of forgiveness.

We can see from this parable that God is not only a God of love but also of mercy. Mercy and love always go together. The psalmist exclaimed, "The mercy of the Lord is from everlasting to everlasting" (Ps. 103:17). Mercy always desires to forgive and never to punish. Mercy pleads for leniency and pardon for the guilty sinner.

God is both a God of justice and a God of mercy. But how can He exercise both in dealing with sinners? Justice requires our sins to be punished, but love pleads for our pardon. How can God both punish and pardon sin?

Praise God that He possesses another divine attribute—wisdom. In His infinite wisdom, stimulated by His holy love, God solved what appears to us to be a great dilemma. He provided a way to save sinners. The cross became the place where both God's justice and His love could be satisfied. On the cross His beloved Son died in the place of guilty sinners, paying in full the penalty for their sins and providing a way of salvation. God did not overlook our sins. Our sins were punished, but that punishment fell on His own perfect Son. "The Lord hath laid on him [Christ] the iniquity of us all" (Isa. 53:6). "Christ died for our sins" (I Cor. 15:3). "Christ . . . suffered for sins, the just for the unjust, that he might bring us to God" (I Pet. 3:18). When Christ died, He said, "It is finished" (John 19:30). What did He mean? He meant that the atonement for our sins was complete. Justice had been satisfied. The price was paid. God's mercy could now be extended to sinful humans!

At the cross both God's justice and mercy were requited. His holiness, which required sin to be punished, was satisfied. And His mercy, which pleaded for our pardon, was also satisfied. It is little wonder that Paul said the cross is "the power of God, and the wisdom of God" (I Cor. 1:24). In response to what was accomplished on the cross, William R. Newell wrote:

> O the love that drew salvation's plan!
> O the grace that bro't it down to man!
> O the mighty gulf that God did span
> At Calvary!

Only the cross could be the answer to our salvation. It alone is the means by which sinful man can approach a holy God. It was what I needed as a small boy. Only at the cross can you and I receive the forgiveness we need to bring us into a right relationship with God. Because of this, Paul exclaimed, "God forbid that I should glory, save in the cross of our Lord Jesus Christ"! (Gal. 6:14).

The cross is God's part of salvation. We had nothing whatsoever to do with it. It was the gracious act of a just and loving God to provide a way of salvation for sinful and guilty humanity. Salvation is, first and foremost, the work of God—the operation of His wisdom, love and grace.

Chapter 2

Salvation—Your Part

If Christ died for us and paid the penalty for our sins, does that mean all people are automatically saved? Isn't there something we must do? If so, what is it? As the Philippian jailer asked Paul and Silas, "What must I do to be saved?" (Acts 16:30). Every searching individual asks this question, whether or not he has heard the Gospel. When a person begins to long for salvation and fellowship with God, his first question naturally is "What must I do?" Unfortunately, many become so concerned about what they need to do that they become blinded to what God has already done for them.

Sinners are not automatically saved on the basis of the fact that Christ died for them. The individual must respond to what has been done. This does not mean that we can do anything to *earn* our salvation, but we must respond in simple faith to what Christ did for us, personally, on the cross.

Our part in salvation then is simple—faith. "By grace are ye saved through faith" (Eph. 2:8). When the Philippian jailer cried out, "Sirs, what must I do to be saved?" (Acts 16:30), Paul and Silas simply told him, "Believe on the Lord Jesus Christ, and thou shalt be saved" (v. 31). So our part in salvation is just simple, childlike, trusting faith. Nothing more is needed, nothing less will suffice, and nothing else will do.

But perhaps another question is forming in your mind: *Just what is faith?* Faith seems to be a hard concept to grasp and harder yet to exercise. Yet it ought to be the simplest thing possible, and in a sense it is. First of all, faith involves knowledge, or understanding. This is true of any form of faith— even that which is exercised in a thousand ways in everyday life. You cannot believe in something you know nothing about. Faith is a response to what we hear or learn. Whenever you hear about something, you either believe it to be the truth or you do not— you either exercise faith in it or you do not. Saving faith requires that you know about the cross and understand, at least to some degree, what Christ accomplished there on your behalf. When a person hears the message that Christ died for his sins, saving faith is not exercised until he grasps the fact that Christ died for *him* and he trusts Christ's work to save him by applying it to his account. You can deposit a lot of money in a bank, but it will do you no good until it is credited to your account. In the same way, you must trust Christ's atonement by acknowledging your spiritual bankruptcy and by crediting His payment to your account.

I will never forget the night when faith became mine. A man of God had explained the Gospel to me clearly, pointing me to the cross and Christ's invitation to come and be saved. But all I could see

13

was my sin and unworthiness. He prayed and I tried to, but I left the meeting that evening in spiritual darkness and misery.

However, after reaching home, when I was on my knees beside my bed, the truth suddenly became clear to me that Jesus Christ had actually paid the penalty for *all* my sins! I understood for the first time the divine plan of salvation—faith had started to grow. I knew now what Christ had done on the cross of Calvary. Such knowledge is the first element of faith.

Faith also involves a decision. Once you understand what Christ did for you on the cross, you must make a choice—either to repent of sin and accept Christ or to reject His work on your behalf. Perhaps you have been raised in a Christian home and have heard Bible teaching all of your life. You still must make a choice about what you will do with this information. To do nothing is really a choice to reject what you have heard.

Accepting Christ, as we have mentioned, involves the decision to repent of sin. Everyone who understands a degree of spiritual truth knows that following Christ means forsaking sin. He who hasn't understood that is not yet enlightened to the point of possessing faith. It is this necessity to repent that keeps many from trusting Christ. What a pity it is that some, who understand fully what salvation is, decide to reject His grace and go on in their sinful way! Such people have not exercised faith, for you must not only understand with your mind but also exercise your will. Faith involves both the intellect and the will. When a person knows that Christ died for him, the only thing that stands between him and salvation is his will. What will your choice be as you gaze at Christ on the cross, paying for the guilt of your sin?

Suppose that you are so ill you are nearly at the point of death. Your relatives learn of a famous doctor who has treated others with the symptoms you have. He is called to your bedside. He diagnoses your problem and prescribes the remedy. The medicine he prescribes is quite expensive, but your relatives secure it, paying the enormous price at great sacrifice. Are you cured because the remedy has been prescribed, purchased and placed beside your bed? Of course not. You must take the remedy provided. If you refuse to do that, you will die. But if you are willing to take the remedy, you will live. In the same way you must accept God's remedy for sin—Christ's finished work on the cross—in order to benefit from it.

Suppose you want to make a trip to Europe by airplane. Your ticket is purchased and is in your hand. You look at the plane on the airport runway, declaring your knowledge of the craft and your confidence in it. But will that get you across the ocean? Certainly not! You must exercise your faith by actually boarding the plane. Only when the faith you claimed to possess moves into action by your stepping on the plane, can you make the crossing— unless the plane fails. In the case of Christ, He cannot fail.

Have you made your decision? Have you understood what Christ has done for you and accepted it? Have you exercised your faith by trusting Him, which included repenting of your sins and sincerely purposing in your heart to follow Him? If not, then you now face this decision. It is the most important decision you will ever make, for it determines your eternal destiny. If you have accepted Christ and repented of your sin, then your salvation is forever sealed.

To add another simple word, faith is just believing the promises of God's Word. His Word says, "As many as received him, to them gave he power to become the sons of God, even to them that believe on his name" (John 1:12). Christ promises, "Him that cometh to me I will in no wise cast out" (6:37). And He has given this invitation: "Come unto me, all ye that labour and are heavy laden, and I will give you rest" (Matt. 11:28). Those who accept His invitation are assured: "God . . . gave his only begotten Son, that whosoever believeth in him should not perish, but have everlasting life" (John 3:16).

Will God keep His word? Will Christ fulfill His promises? Our salvation depends on the trustworthiness of God. Hence, faith is, in the final and simplest analysis, believing the promises of God's Word, the Bible. If we do not cling to His promises, we can have no sure hope. But since His Word is sure, our salvation is secure.

Faith is a matter of clinging to the crucified Christ. You may not understand all of the spiritual significance or the theological explanations about the atonement, but you know that Christ paid the penalty for your sins and that this alone is your hope of salvation. Therefore, you cling to that crucified Saviour in earnest, simple faith. Augustus M. Toplady expressed it beautifully when he wrote:

> Rock of ages, cleft for me,
> Let me hide myself in Thee;
> Let the water and the blood,
> From Thy wounded side which flowed,
> Be of sin the double cure,
> Save from wrath and make me pure.
>
> Could my tears forever flow,
> Could my zeal no languor know,
> These for sin could not atone—
> Thou must save, and Thou alone:
> In my hand no price I bring,
> Simply to Thy cross I cling.

The last line expresses very well what constitutes true, saving faith.

A Christian who was having serious doubts concerning his salvation once confided his difficulties to me. He was very troubled. My counsel to him was that whenever those doubts recurred, he should simply say to himself, *My one hope of salvation is Christ and His work on the cross. To Him I will cling for salvation, come what may. And if I go to hell, I will go there trusting Christ.* I knew that no spiritually enlightened person, such as this man was, could think for one minute that he could go to hell trusting Christ. Try this method yourself when you are tempted to doubt God's glorious salvation.

Some may be tempted to delay trusting Christ because they think they are too sinful. But when we

17

acknowledge our sinfulness to Christ, He accepts us just as we are. The words of a hymn by Charlotte Elliott express this well:

> Just as I am, without one plea
> But that Thy blood was shed for me,
> And that Thou bidd'st me come to Thee,
> O Lamb of God, I come! I come!
>
> Just as I am, Thou wilt receive,
> Wilt welcome, pardon, cleanse, relieve;
> Because Thy promise I believe,
> O Lamb of God, I come! I come!

Chapter 3

Your Assurance of Salvation

Is assurance of salvation possible? Some religious people say that it is impossible for a person to know for sure whether or not he actually possesses eternal life until he dies and stands before the Judgment Seat of God. They are quite surprised—sometimes even indignant—at the testimony of those Christians who say they are positive that they are saved. But even some true Christians do not have assurance of their salvation and think it is impossible to attain such assurance in this life.

If being a Christian meant doing my best to follow Christ but never knowing at the end of a day whether I was any nearer to heaven or to hell than I was the day before, Christianity would indeed be a poor religion. If Christ asked me to follow Him and to trust Him but in return gave me no assurance of my eternal destiny, then He would not be much of a Saviour. However, many people have just such a concept of Christ and of Christianity.

But is this the Bible's concept? Does the New Testament tell us that followers of Christ must grope through life in darkness and uncertainty, never knowing until they die whether they are saved or lost? Is that the best God and the Christian life can offer? Is that the best message we can offer to hopeless men and women? Is the message of the Gospel one of doubt and uncertainty?

No, of course not! The message of the Bible is one of assurance. It is the believer's privilege to know that he has eternal life while he is living. The Apostle John wrote to the early believers: "These things have I written unto you that believe on the name of the Son of God; that ye may know that ye have eternal life, and that ye may believe on the name of the Son of God" (I John 5:13). John wrote this entire epistle so that those believers who read it would be assured that they possessed eternal life. To deny the possibility of the believer's assurance of salvation would be to deny the message of the First Epistle of John—to say that it was written in vain. And that would be an insult to the Holy Spirit, who inspired John to write it. To those who say it is presumptuous for a Christian to say he knows that he is saved, we should reply: "Is it presumptuous to believe God? On the contrary, it is presumptuous not to believe God and to make Him a liar."

Christ promises eternal life as a present possession to all who will put their trust in Him. Therefore, to doubt that you have eternal life after you have trusted Christ for salvation is actually to consider Him untrue to His promises.

But how may a person know that he has eternal life? Three sources of this assurance are (1) the change that has taken place in his life, (2) the testimony of the Word of God and (3) the inward witness of the Holy Spirit.

The first source of assurance will be changes that occur in the person's life. The Apostle Paul declared, "If any man be in Christ, he is a new creature: old things are passed away; behold, all things are become new" (II Cor. 5:17). When an individual genuinely trusts Jesus Christ for salvation, a divine transformation takes place in that person's life. The nature of Christ is imparted to that person so that he becomes one of the "partakers of the divine nature" (II Pet. 1:4). This new nature naturally results in new desires, new likes, new dislikes, new goals, new motives, new thoughts. The entire inward disposition of his life has been changed.

Not only is this change apparent to the individual himself, but his outward behavior will also likely appear different to those around him. His character will be changed. Often a change in disposition is noticed. There might even be a change in the person's vocabulary and in the topics of his conversation.

After I was saved, I experienced times of doubt about the genuineness of my salvation. But I was certain of one thing—I had been changed. My whole outlook on life was different. I had a real desire to serve the Lord and to pray. I longed for fellowship with Him. I wanted to learn more about His Word. I enjoyed being with other Christians. I loved the singing of Gospel songs. I enjoyed going to meetings to hear the Word taught. All of this had been foreign to my nature before I became a Christian. Before,

21

those things had little, if any, appeal to me. Most remarkable of all was the change of vocabulary that took place after my conversion. My language had been profane; I hardly knew how to express myself without using evil language. But after I believed in the Lord Jesus, to my own surprise, that kind of language just faded away.

Furthermore, although I was young, I had developed a number of evil habits, such as chewing and smoking tobacco. I seemed to crave tobacco. But after I was saved, that craving disappeared. Although the desire occasionally returned later, it was never strong enough to overcome me. I am not saying that because a person may be tempted to use tobacco, he is not a Christian. The point I am making is that when one does meet the Lord, there will be changes within him, particularly in his desires.

If you can honestly say that a change has taken place in your life—altering your desires, affections and inward nature—you may rest assured that such a change has been made by the Spirit of God and is a sign that you are saved. When a person becomes a Christian, he is "born again." Birth is the demonstration of physical life. The new birth is the demonstration of new life, or spiritual life. A new birth and a new life naturally mean that you now have a new inner nature. If you are conscious of a new nature within, it is an evidence that you are born of God. Of course, your old nature is still there, and at times it conflicts with your new nature. But this very conflict is an evidence that you are a Christian.

Paul said, "The flesh lusteth against the Spirit,

and the Spirit against the flesh: and these are contrary the one to the other: so that ye cannot do the things that ye would" (Gal. 5:17). If such a conflict is going on in you, it is a clear sign that a new life and a new nature have been implanted within you. Your old nature, which is called the "flesh," fights against your new nature, which is indwelt by the Spirit. So if you have accepted Christ as your Saviour and if, as a result, you are conscious that a change has taken place within you, this is an evidence that you are a true Christian—that you have been saved and made a child of God forever.

Our second source of assurance is the Word of God. The believer can have assurance of his salvation because of what the Word says. The testimony of the Bible is the testimony of God Himself; therefore, whatever the Scriptures say is absolutely sure.

In John 1:12 we read: "As many as received him, to them gave he power [the right] to become the sons of God, even to them that believe on his name." Here is a clear statement in God's Word that everyone who receives Jesus, or believes on Him for salvation, positively becomes a child of God. In Acts 13:39 we read: "By him all that believe are justified from all things." To be justified means "to be declared just," or to be declared free from the guilt of sin. Everyone who believes in Jesus can be assured that he is justified from all things because the Word of God plainly says so. What better assurance could you have?

The Lord Jesus Christ promised, "He that heareth my word, and believeth . . . hath everlasting life, and shall not come into condemnation; but is passed from death unto life" (John 5:24). So if you have placed your faith in the Son of God as your Saviour, then, on the basis of His promise, you have eternal life and will never face judgment. Whether you "feel" saved or not doesn't really matter. What matters is what God's Word says. You can always trust God's Word, but you cannot always trust your feelings.

Many believers doubt their salvation and relationship to God because they do not feel saved. But they should accept the assurance of their salvation on the basis of God's promises. The only question we need to ask is, "Have I met the condition of God's promises?" That condition is faith in the finished work of Christ. If you are trusting the finished work of Christ for your salvation, then God says that you are saved. What better basis of assurance could you have than the Word of God?

When Jesus said to the sinful woman in the house of Simon, "Thy sins are forgiven" (Luke 7:48), was it presumptuous for her to go out and say, "I know that all of my sins have been forgiven"? Instead, wouldn't it have been presumptuous for her to say she doubted that her sins were forgiven? In the same way a Christian can say, "My sins are forgiven, and I know I am saved" because God plainly states in His Word, "In whom [Christ] we have redemption through his blood, the forgiveness of sins, according to the riches of his grace" (Eph. 1:7). Of the Ephesian Christians the Apostle Paul said, "God for Christ's sake hath forgiven you" (4:32).

God's promise is "Whosoever shall call upon the name of the Lord shall be saved" (Rom. 10:13). If you have asked the Lord Jesus Christ to save you, either He has saved you or God's promise is untrue. In I John 5:11,12 we read: "This is the record, that God hath given to us eternal life, and this life is in his Son. He that hath the Son hath life; and he that hath not the Son of God hath not life." If you have trusted the Lord Jesus Christ, you have eternal life. We can see that God's Word contains many promises that give us assurance of salvation here and now.

If Satan should cause you to doubt that your sins are forgiven, tell him, "God says that my sins are forgiven because I have believed in the Lord Jesus Christ, and I believe Him." Then if Satan should lead you to think, *Well, perhaps I don't believe in Him,* just say, "If I have never believed in Him before, I accept Him and believe in Him right now." Then go on your way rejoicing, knowing that your sins are forgiven and that you are a child of God on the basis of His written promises.

Dr. R. A. Torrey has illustrated this point quite well: Suppose that you are sentenced to a term of imprisonment but that your friends are able to secure a pardon for you. The legal document announcing your pardon is brought to you. You read it and know that you are pardoned because the document says so, but the news is so good and so sudden that you are dazed by it.

Someone comes to you and asks, "Are you pardoned?"

You answer, "Yes, I am pardoned."

Then he asks, "Do you feel pardoned?"

You reply, "No, I don't feel pardoned. It's so sudden and wonderful that I can hardly believe it!"

Then he says to you, "But how can you know that you are pardoned if you don't feel like it?"

You hold out the document and say, "This says so."

Eventually, after you read the document again and again and believe it, you would not only know that you are pardoned because the document says so, you would also feel it.

The Bible is God's authoritative document. It declares that everyone who believes in Jesus is justified, has everlasting life and is a child of God. If anyone asks if your sins are all forgiven, just reply, "Yes, I know they are because God says so." You may not feel it yet, but if you keep meditating on God's Word and believing what it says, you will feel it.

The third source of assurance of the believer's salvation is the inner witness of the Holy Spirit. The Bible says, "The Spirit itself [Himself] beareth witness with our spirit, that we are the children of God" (Rom. 8:16). Actually, what some would call the "feeling" of salvation is not human emotion at all. It is the inner voice of the Holy Spirit, bearing witness to our spirits that we are children of God. It is not a human emotion but a divine knowledge. The Holy Spirit brings to our inner consciousness the vivid assurance that we are saved.

Of course, the Holy Spirit brings that assurance

to us primarily through the Word of God. Yet in countries where many are unable to read and write, the Holy Spirit has brought the assurance of salvation, in remarkable ways, even to illiterate people. He was sent into our hearts to be our Comforter, and one of His main messages of comfort is to assure us that we are saved. As a Christian reads the Word of God and meditates on it with an open heart, the Holy Spirit takes its truths and implants them in his life, bearing witness to the fact that the believer belongs to Christ.

This inner witness of the Holy Spirit is further strengthened and deepened as we fellowship with God in prayer. Prayer is not only petition but also communion. Not only do we speak to God, but God (through His Holy Spirit) speaks to us. So, if you are troubled with doubts about your salvation, you should not only study the Word of God but also go to God in prayer. As you pray, the Holy Spirit will assure you that you are a child of God. A Christian who neglects his prayer life may soon begin to feel that he isn't saved, because it is through prayer that the Holy Spirit communicates that assurance to us.

Do not think that you must go through life wondering whether you are saved or lost. Changes in your life, the testimony of God's Word and the inner witness of the Holy Spirit all unite to bring the true Christian a definite assurance that he is saved for time and eternity. When doubts persist, look again to the Christ of the cross and say, "He died for my sins. He paid my penalty. He promised that if I would trust Him as my substitute, He would save me. I have trusted Him. Now I depend on Him to keep His promise."

New believers sometimes make the mistake of becoming despondent and feeling unsaved when the fervency of their first love for Christ begins to wane. We need to remember that our human emotions can change with the state of our health, with the weather or with the circumstances in which we find ourselves. But Jesus Christ never changes— He is the same yesterday, today and forever!

Chapter 4

Your Fellowship With God

After you become God's child, the greatest privilege a human being can have is yours—fellowship with Almighty God. How is fellowship with God possible for a sinful human being? It is possible only on the basis of the cross. At the cross a holy God and a sinful human can meet, because it was there that He dealt with our sin.

In the Old Testament, Moses was instructed to erect a tabernacle in which God would dwell among His people (see Ex. 25-27). In that tabernacle Moses was to build a "most holy" place where he was to put what was called the "mercy seat." The mercy seat was made of pure gold, and once each year the blood of atonement was sprinkled on it. God told His people that He would meet them at that blood-sprinkled mercy seat. He could meet the nation of Israel, in the person of their high priest, at the mercy seat because the blood of atonement (which He promised to accept) had been sprinkled on it in their behalf. The blood of atonement made a meeting between God and man possible. So it is with the blood of the cross.

Fellowship with God is possible because of the

cross and because of our faith in the blood that was shed there as an atonement for our sins. In the Book of Hebrews we read: "Having therefore, brethren, boldness to enter into the holiest by the blood of Jesus, by a new and living way, . . . and having an high priest over the house of God; let us draw near with a true heart in full assurance of faith" (10:19-22). The Old Testament tabernacle was a picture of what Christ would later accomplish for us by His death on the cross. He became our high priest, and His blood covered our sins and allowed us to come into the presence of a holy God.

In another place in the same epistle we read: "Seeing then that we have a great high priest, that is passed into the heavens, Jesus the Son of God, let us . . . therefore come boldly unto the throne of grace, that we may obtain mercy, and find grace to help in time of need" (4:14,16). On the basis of the cross and our faith in Christ, we are able to have fellowship with God.

How is this fellowship with God cultivated? It is developed by communication through prayer. On a human level, as you visit with a person and spend time with him, your acquaintance with him grows and your fellowship deepens. The more time you spend together, the richer your friendship becomes. The same is true of our fellowship with God. As far as God is concerned, the way is open for fellowship with His children. We must be sure that nothing within us hinders that fellowship with Him.

This fellowship with God is also cultivated through reading His Word. When we pray, we talk to God.

When we read the Word, we allow God to talk to us. Thus, our fellowship with God is developed when we spend time praying and studying His Word.

How can we continually maintain our fellowship with God? Sin breaks our fellowship. Therefore, we need to purpose in our hearts to avoid sin. But when we do sin, we must confess it and forsake it as soon as we become aware of it. That will restore the fellowship. As David said, "A broken and a contrite heart, O God, thou wilt not despise" (Ps. 51:17). Before writing this, David had been guilty of adultery and murder. His fellowship with God had been so completely broken that he cried out to God, "Cast me not away from thy presence; and take not thy holy spirit from me. Restore unto me the joy of thy salvation; and uphold me with thy free spirit" (vv. 11,12). When God saw his brokenness of heart and heard his confession of sin, He immediately restored David to His fellowship.

When you realize that you have sinned against God, go to Him immediately. Confess the sin by naming it specifically, and ask Him to forgive you and restore you to fellowship. He will be true to His Word to do just that.

Fellowship with God is indispensable in the Christian life. Without it you cannot experience the true joy of the Lord, which He wants you to have. Christ told His disciples, "These things have I spoken unto you, that my joy might remain in you, and that your joy might be full" (John 15:11). Joy and rejoicing is a frequent topic in the New Testament, because we know the risen Saviour. Peter

31

said, "Whom having not seen, ye love; in whom, though now ye see him not, yet believing, ye rejoice with joy unspeakable and full of glory" (I Pet. 1:8). The Apostle Paul wrote to the Philippian Christians: "Rejoice in the Lord alway: and again I say, Rejoice" (Phil. 4:4). And to the Romans he wrote: "For the kingdom of God is not meat and drink; but righteousness, and peace, and joy in the Holy Ghost" (Rom. 14:17).

The fact that God wants His children to be happy and joyful is emphasized throughout the New Testament. But if your fellowship with God is broken, you lose the joy of salvation. Happy Christians are those who live in close fellowship with God—those who pray and read God's Word. In the marriage relationship, joy results from fellowship between the husband and the wife. When that fellowship is broken, the joy is gone. In a home, joy results from fellowship and harmony between all the members of the family. When that fellowship is broken, the joy of the home is destroyed.

Fellowship with God is indispensable for a life of victory over sin and Satan. Spiritual strength comes from vital fellowship with God. The Christian who backslides does so because he begins to neglect his relationship with God. If you fail to live in fellowship with God by praying and reading His Word, you will begin to drift away from the Lord. Soon you will be an easy target for Satan, the world and your old sin nature. These enemies are too strong for us to defeat in our own strength. We must derive strength from the Lord, and that comes as we fellowship with

Him daily. Satan understands our weakness, and this is why he tries so hard to keep us from praying or studying God's Word. He is very subtle in the good things he brings our way to keep us from prayer and God's Word.

Fellowship with God is also indispensable if we are to bear fruit for the Lord. In John 15, Jesus used the union of the vine and the branch to illustrate the relationship between Himself and the Christian. He pointed out that a branch can bear fruit only if it is attached to the vine and draws its life from the vine. Then He made the spiritual parallel: "Abide in me, and I in you. As the branch cannot bear fruit of itself, except it abide in the vine; no more can ye, except ye abide in me. . . . For without me ye can do nothing" (vv. 4,5). A branch that is not united with the vine and does not draw its sap from the vine will soon be dead and useless. Similarly, if we believers fail to live in constant fellowship with Christ, our lives will become lifeless and barren. If you are teaching a Sunday school class or are the leader of a youth group, remember that you will accomplish nothing apart from Christ. Your work might look successful to others, but no lasting fruit will remain. Any service for Christ must be done according to His will and in His power by total dependence on Him.

In practical terms, how can we maintain constant fellowship with God? While we must avoid dead formalism in our prayer life, a few simple suggestions will be helpful. First, begin the day with thanksgiving and prayer. Think of some of the blessings God has given you, and thank Him for them. Then ask God to give you strength for victory over the temptations you will meet during the day. Anticipate your battles in the morning, and claim His overcoming grace. Don't let the urgency of the day's business cheat you out of an unhurried and quiet time with the Lord.

Second, stop during the day to communicate with your Lord. When He gives you some unexpected joy or blessing, take a moment to thank Him for it. When you realize temptation is near, ask for His help. Talk naturally with Him as a loving child would talk to his earthly father. A few moments alone with God throughout the day will keep you calm and triumphant in the midst of life's care and turmoil.

Third, end the day with thanksgiving and prayer. Review the blessings and victories of your day, and thank God for them in detail. If you failed during the day, confess your sins honestly to the Lord. He will then forgive and cleanse you. However, you need not wait until the end of the day to confess your sins. They should be confessed the moment you become aware of them. This would be a good time, though, to ask the Lord to examine your life and point out any sins of which you may be unaware. Then you can confess and forsake them.

Prayer is your avenue of communion with God. Fellowship with Him is not only a privilege; it is also indispensable for a joyful, victorious, successful, fruitful Christian life.

Chapter 5

Your Fellowship With God's People

The company a person keeps has a great deal to do with the character he develops. A person's spiritual life, as well as his intellectual and social life, is helped or hindered by the companions he chooses. It is important, therefore, for every Christian to deliberately cultivate Christian fellowship and to choose mature, godly friends for his intimate companions.

The Book of Proverbs, one of the most practical books of the Old Testament, says much about friends and companions. For example: "He that walketh with wise men shall be wise: but a companion of fools shall be destroyed" (13:20); "Make no friendship with an angry man; and with a furious man thou shalt not go: lest thou learn his ways, and get a snare to thy soul" (22:24,25); "Confidence in an unfaithful man in time of trouble is like a broken tooth, and a foot out of joint" (25:19).

No matter who we are or how strong or mature we may be, we are all affected by others. Since we are social beings, we require fellowship and companionship. Therefore, we should choose, cherish and cultivate godly Christian friendships. For your

35

most intimate friends, you will want to select a few believers who have similar spiritual desires and goals to yours. You will want friends who can encourage you to grow spiritually. On the other hand, you will want to avoid being close companions with those whom you know would be harmful to you spiritually and morally. You should not completely withdraw from unsaved people, but they should not be your most intimate friends. If you find that a friendship is detrimental to you, then break it off.

Don't think that the Christian life is lonely, without any good fellowship or social relationships. Not at all! The richest friendship in the world is found among Christians. The social oneness and harmony among the Christians of the first few centuries after Christ greatly impressed the ungodly rulers. It even caused the Roman emperor Constantine to endorse the Christian faith and proclaim it the official religion of his empire. Unbelievers among whom those early Christians lived could not comprehend their love and devotion for one another and the pure fellowship that existed among them.

In Christ, social and class distinctions and prejudices are swept away, and men and women become conscious of their oneness in Him. On some mission fields I have seen members of tribes and races that had previously hated each other work, live and pray together like brothers. In North Africa I have seen embittered Jews and arrogant Arabs, made one in Christ, enjoying the holiest fellowship together. People in America who hated each other for years have become intimate friends after they were saved.

Christian fellowship even transcends language barriers. An American Christian once met a European in a London city park. Both were feeling somewhat lonely. As one looked at the other, each somehow knew that the other was a Christian, and this mutual understanding drew them together. As they moved closer to each other, one of them exclaimed, "Hallelujah!" and the other reponded with a resounding "Amen!" With only these two words, both were uplifted and encouraged by their contact and fellowship. There is a common bond that draws Christians together and a common language that transcends linguistic vocabularies.

As one hymnwriter expressed it:

> Blest be the tie that binds
>   Our hearts in Christian love!
> The fellowship of kindred minds
>   Is like to that above.
>
> Before our Father's throne
>   We pour our ardent prayers;
> Our fears, our hopes, our aims are one,
>   Our comforts and our cares.
>
> We share our mutual woes,
>   Our mutual burdens bear;
> And often for each other flows
>   The sympathizing tear.
>
> —John Fawcett

T. J. Bach, well-known missionary and Christian leader for many years, very aptly defined "fellowship" as "two fellows in the same ship." Two fellows on the same ship, out on the ocean, away from everything else, are going to have a lot in common. They must work together, they must weather storms together, and they must share their provisions. A disagreement between them would be tragic, perhaps even deadly.

Satan is very busy trying to disrupt the fellowship of Christians. He tries to do this even among those who agree on the basic truths of the Christian faith. He tries to stir up division within churches, among the members. One member will disagree with another—even over a minor issue—and the war is on! He tries to cause strife among Christian leaders and workers. He loves to create trouble between Christian neighbors. He tries to divide the Christian home by producing arguments and a lack of forgiveness among family members. He delights to end a friendship by causing one person to be hurt by the other. He tries to mar the fellowship of Christians everywhere.

Broken fellowship among God's people is a tragedy. Our Saviour is grieved by it, for He prayed for His followers that they "all may be one; as thou, Father, art in me, and I in thee, that they also may be one in us: that the world may believe" (John 17:21). The Holy Spirit is grieved by it, for by Him we have all been baptized into one Body (I Cor. 12:13). And in Ephesians 4:30-32 we read: "Grieve not the holy Spirit of God, whereby ye are sealed unto the day of redemption. Let all bitterness, and wrath, and anger, and clamour, and evil speaking, be put away

38

from you, with all malice: and be ye kind one to another, tenderhearted, forgiving one another, even as God for Christ's sake hath forgiven you." You lose the joy of the Lord when you allow sin to break your fellowship with other believers. Your prayers are hindered, your testimony is weakened, and your spiritual power is diminished. Broken fellowship takes a serious toll.

Christian fellowship needs to be cultivated and guarded. One of the best ways to do this is to become involved in a good local church. You may need to visit several churches before you find the right one, but then you should make that church your home. If you move constantly from one church to another, it will be difficult for you to establish any genuine fellowship. Invite the people in your church to your home for informal social companionship. Plan picnics and other activities that include other Christians and their families. Soon you will begin to develop friendships with many individuals and families. It will become natural to pray for them and to ask them to pray for you.

One excellent way to cultivate a friendship is to find a "prayer partner." You will probably want to select someone who is close to your own age and who has a desire to grow spiritually. You will want to share your needs and problems with that person. It is best to have a fixed time—probably once a week—to share and pray together by yourselves.

Of course, you shouldn't think that every contact with a Christian friend has to be centered around something spiritual. You need to develop in all areas

39

of your life—socially, intellectually, physically and emotionally as well as spiritually. Christian fellowship should be versatile and universal. It could include eating together, enjoying recreation together, helping one another in material ways, traveling together or just chatting together.

Remember that the responsibility for cultivating such fellowship is yours as much as the other person's. Prize and guard your friendships. Here are some sensible ways to do that: Don't be selfish; learn to overlook small faults—we all have them; don't betray a confidence; don't repeat what you hear others say about your friend unless it's a true statement that you need to share in love to help him grow.

Listen to Solomon's counsel about friendship: "A friend loveth at all times" (Prov. 17:17); "He that covereth a transgression seeketh love; but he that repeateth a matter separateth very friends" (v. 9); "The words of a talebearer are as wounds" (18:8); "A brother offended is harder to be won than a strong city" (v. 19); "A talebearer revealeth secrets: but he that is of a faithful spirit concealeth the matter" (11:13).

Solomon also warned us about spending too much time with a friend so that we become a nuisance: "Withdraw thy foot from thy neighbour's house; lest he be weary of thee, and so hate thee" (25:17).

When anything occurs to strain the relationship between you and your friend, go to him quickly and discuss it frankly so that the problem can be resolved. If you have been at fault, say so and ask your friend to forgive you. If the other person has been at fault, forgive him—even if he doesn't ask you to. In most cases, you are probably both at fault. Above all, do not hold a grudge against your friend. Instead, forgive him and settle the matter so that your friendship can continue. Christian friends are too valuable to lose and too hard to replace. They are, in fact, indispensable to your spiritual life.

When you became a follower of Jesus Christ, if you had to give up some (or perhaps the majority) of your old friends, don't be dismayed. You will find better friends in Christ than you ever had before. You will find that most Christian friends will be true and faithful. Of course, you may find some exceptions, for there are hypocrites even among Christians.

My Christian friends have stood with me during good times and troubled times, while unsaved friends have forgotten me. The unbeliever is, after all, a selfish person. But the believer has the love of God and the compassion of Christ in his heart. A self-centered person will think only of himself, but a Christ-centered person will think of others. Actually, those people who stand between you and the Lord are not really your friends; they are your worst enemies. Any person who will keep another person from serving God is a foe, not a friend.

So, if you want true friends who will help you in every way, seek Christian friends. If you want to succeed and grow in your Christian life and to be a testimony for Christ, cultivate Christian companionship. You may fall if you walk alone. But if you walk with other believers, they will support and strengthen you.

One Saturday evening many years ago, I was very discouraged. I got together with a close Christian friend, and we spent the evening visiting and praying together. I said nothing to him about my discouragement. But, when we parted, I was so encouraged that I almost felt like going out and looking for some more trouble!

A couple of weeks later, we met again. One of the first things my friend said to me was "You know, I was so discouraged when we met that night that I almost felt like giving up. But after we spent that evening together, my faith and courage were renewed and revived. I was lifted up. I wanted to tell you about it."

This is a perfect example of the value of Christian fellowship! Two discouraged Christians spent a few hours together, and both were lifted out of their discouragement. Cultivate a few true, intimate Christian friends. When you are discouraged or troubled, seek their fellowship.

Fellowship with God's people is one of the best benefits of the Christian life. Be sure you take advantage of it.

Chapter 6

Your Spiritual Diet

In the Word of God, spiritual life is compared to physical life. Both must be sustained by correct and careful nourishment. Our new life was imparted to us in a new birth when we trusted the Saviour. If a newborn baby were left without proper care and nourishment, could he be expected to grow and develop? Of course not! He would die. Likewise, our spiritual life must be properly nurtured and nourished if we are to grow as a Christian. *Becoming* a Christian is a matter of birth (the new birth); *being* a Christian is a matter of growth. "Grow in grace," Peter exhorted, "and in the knowledge of our Lord and Saviour Jesus Christ" (II Pet. 3:18).

All of life depends on food for growth. So God, in His wisdom and grace, provided richly for the care and feeding of our spiritual life through His Word, the Bible. It contains a balanced diet, providing everything necessary for health and growth. It contains pure milk, sweet honey, living bread, the water of life, strong meat and all kinds of rich fruits. (All of these items are used in Scripture to describe the Bible.)

Food will be of no use to you on the shelf. You

must read your Bible. Read it diligently, honestly trying to understand what it says and means. Careless reading will not promote growth. People often complain that they cannot understand the Bible. Perhaps they have not really tried. However, if you have made a diligent effort, do not be concerned about what you don't understand. Start with what you do understand, and put it into practice in your life. The more you study the Word and hear it taught by others and the longer you walk with the Lord, the more you will understand. The Holy Spirit will be your guide as you learn. If you begin with the New Testament, possibly with the Book of Mark, you will be amazed at how much you comprehend.

Another aid to understanding the Bible is to use an up-to-date English version. Several excellent translations are available, including the *New American Standard Bible*, the *New International Version*, *The New Berkeley Version*, *The Amplified Bible* and *The New King James Version*. I would recommend that you secure at least one of these helpful editions and become thoroughly familiar with it.

You need to read your Bible regularly and systematically. You normally wouldn't go without food for days at a time; neither should you neglect your spiritual nourishment. To do so will stunt your growth and development. It is best to set aside a regular time each day for Bible reading and prayer. A good goal is to have no less than 15 minutes of Bible reading daily. Many believers spend an hour or more a day studying the Bible.

No matter how busy you may be, don't neglect your time in God's Word. It's a tragedy when a person becomes so busy making a living that he cannot take time to eat! If you want to be a strong and mature Christian, you must spend time "feeding" on the Bible and communicating with God. In prayer we talk to God. In the Bible God talks to us. The two go together.

But it's not enough just to read and study the Bible; you must obey it. No one can really understand the Scriptures unless they are willing to obey its injunctions. The Lord Jesus said, "If any man is willing to do His will, he shall know of the teaching" (John 7:17, NASB). When you obey what you know, that prepares you to understand more and take the next step of obedience. It is amazing how quickly you begin to lose your desire for Bible reading when you openly disobey what God has told you to do. Your fellowship with Him is broken, and you feel uncomfortable reading His Word.

A friend who had greatly influenced my life once told me, "Years ago I made up my mind that as I read the Bible, I would—by God's grace—attempt to do everything it commanded me." That remark explained to me why he was so Christlike and had so much spiritual power. He let the Word of God accomplish its purpose in him.

It will be helpful to read your Bible prayerfully, asking the Spirit of God to reveal its truths to you and to apply them to your life. The Bible is God's inspired Word, and it cannot be understood with the natural mind alone. First Corinthians 2:12-15

45

tells us, "Now we have received, not the spirit of the world, but the spirit which is of God; that we might know the things that are freely given to us of God. Which things also we speak, not in the words which man's wisdom teacheth, but which the Holy Ghost teacheth. . . . But the natural man receiveth not the things of the Spirit of God: for they are foolishness unto him: neither can he know them, because they are spiritually discerned. But he that is spiritual judgeth all things." Only those who are guided by the Holy Spirit can grasp spiritual truth. And the Bible is, of course, primarily a book of spiritual truth.

If you pray as David did when you study the Word, you will find you can better comprehend its truths: "Open thou mine eyes, that I may behold wondrous things out of thy law" (Ps. 119:18). Whenever you read the Bible, ask the Holy Spirit to give you the power to discern and grasp the meaning. If you encounter a difficult passage, ask Him to give you the explanation. Jesus promised, "When he, the Spirit of truth, is come, he will guide you into all truth" (John 16:13). God is the author of the Bible; therefore, He is its best teacher and interpreter.

Commentaries on the Bible definitely have value, but you will learn more through the direction of the Holy Spirit than from all the books ever written about the Bible. Even the newest believer in Christ, who might not be able to understand the scholarly commentaries, is given the privilege of having the Spirit's assistance and, hence, being able to understand the Scriptures. This is why it is necessary to read the Bible prayerfully and with a mind open to the direction of God's Spirit.

If you carry a small New Testament or a pocket edition of the Bible with you all the time, you can read it during time that is usually wasted. You can read it while you're riding a bus or plane, while waiting for appointments, while taking a break from work—anytime you find a few spare minutes. These moments of reading will be as refreshing to your spiritual life as a snack is to your physical body during the day.

You will want to memorize verses from your Bible. David long ago declared, "Thy word have I hid in mine heart, that I might not sin against thee" (Ps. 119:11). The *New American Standard Bible* translates this verse: "Thy word I have treasured in my heart, that I may not sin against Thee." There is great value in memorizing the Word of God. First of all, as David stated, it will help keep us from sinning. During a time of temptation, if you have memorized a verse that applies to the situation, the Holy Spirit can remind you of it. The convicting power of that verse may be enough to keep you from committing a sinful act. God's Word is a powerful restraining force.

Scripture committed to memory will also equip you to witness to others. Our words and arguments may not be very effective, but God always uses and honors His Word. When human urging and reasoning fail, the Word of God remains "quick [living], and powerful, and sharper than any twoedged sword . . . and is a discerner of the thoughts and intents of the heart" (Heb. 4:12). Anyone who attempts to witness without knowing God's Word will be at a great disadvantage. We especially need to use the Scriptures when we must exhort fellow Christians. It is God's Word that will convince and convict them of their wrongdoing. It is important to memorize Scripture for those times when you may not have a Bible with you.

There are many ways to memorize Scripture. One simple suggestion is to memorize one verse selected from your daily Bible reading—perhaps the verse that means the most to you that day. Underline it in your Bible or Testament and review it at various times during the day. Also keep reviewing those previously learned. Constant repetition is the secret of memorization. (If one verse per day seems beyond your time and ability, start with less.) A good method for reviewing the memorized verses is to type or print them on little cards and carry them with you. Then you can review them during spare minutes.

A number of Scripture memory aids have been devised. Basically, these are lists of verses organized in a logical sequence. They usually include some mechanical aids, such as cards, packets and filing systems, to help you. The Navigators and the Bible Memory Association have produced some excellent materials. Back to the Bible also has available *Bible Themes Memory Plan*. The personnel at your local Christian bookstore could assist you in finding helpful material to use. Begin now to memorize God's Word, for it will yield rich spiritual dividends.

In addition to reading the Scriptures daily for devotional and inspirational purposes, every person who wants to succeed in being a real Christian must study the Bible. Finding time for this may be a problem, but you should set aside some regular time for this purpose. As R. A. Torrey once said, "There is nothing more important for the development of the spiritual life of the Christian than regular, systematic Bible study."

Our spiritual health, our growth, our strength, our victory over sin, our soundness in doctrine, our joy and peace in Christ, our cleansing from sin, our fitness for service—all depend on the study of the Word of God. It has well been said, "A Bible that is falling apart usually belongs to a person who isn't."

One method of Bible study is to do a chapter analysis. Select a book of the Bible you want to study. Read it through, chapter by chapter, until you begin to master the contents of each chapter. Dr. R. A. Torrey favored this method, which includes reading each chapter through several times and then answering questions such as these:

1. What is the principal subject of the chapter? (State the principal contents in a single phrase or sentence.)
2. What is the truth most clearly taught and most emphasized in the chapter?
3. What verse is most meaningful to you?
4. Who are the principal people mentioned?

5. What does the chapter teach about Jesus Christ?
6. What new truth have you learned from the chapter?
7. What have you resolved to do as a result of studying this chapter?

You can master book after book of the Bible this way.

Another method of studying the Bible is to use a topical approach. This was the chief method the famous preacher D. L. Moody used when he studied the Scriptures. It is a very simple and valuable method. It requires a few reference books, but they are easy to obtain. You will need a topical Bible, such as *Nave's Topical Bible,* and/or a good concordance, such as *Young's Analytical Concordance* or *Strong's Exhaustive Concordance.* A chain-reference Bible or a study Bible will also contain valuable helps. (These books can be secured by contacting your local Christian bookstore or your church library.) Even the marginal references of any good Bible will be of great assistance in this method of study.

Use your topical Bible or concordance to study all the Scripture passages you can find on a certain topic, such as the Holy Spirit, sin, grace, the blood of Christ, justification, faith, repentance, the new birth, the resurrections (of Christ, of believers, of all), the love of God, our love (to God, to Christians, to all people), the coming of Christ, heaven, hell. You can probably think of other topics that interest you. Using any other aids you have, see what additional information you can find on your chosen topic.

The topical method of Bible study is a good method to use if you are preparing to teach a class or share a message on a certain topic. By using this method, you can make an exhaustive study of virtually any Bible doctrine or theme.

Another method of Bible study is to do a book analysis. (This is sometimes called the synthetic method.) Dr. James M. Gray, longtime president of Moody Bible Institute, loved to use this method. This method allows you to master the contents of any book of the Bible. Choose the book you want to study (you may want to start with one of the shorter New Testament epistles) and read it several times until you have a good overview of the book and what it is teaching. After the second reading, begin to look for the main theme of the book. At the next reading, note how the theme is developed. Then in subsequent readings outline the book, keeping in mind the central theme. You may want to refer to the questions used in the chapter analysis to help you discover the key elements in each chapter. But you must also keep in mind how each chapter relates to the others.

Stay in one book until you feel you have mastered it. Then go on to another. During the course of your Christian life, you may study every book of the Bible in this fashion. It can be done; in fact, it's not as difficult as you may think.

Another method of study is the character method.

In this study you will learn all you can about individuals in the Bible. Here again your topical Bible or one of the special Bibles referred to in the topical method will be invaluable. Choose a Bible character and study all that the Bible says about that individual. You might want to start with one of the following: Noah, Abraham, Lot, Jacob, Joseph, Moses, Joshua, Gideon, Samson, Ruth, Samuel, Saul, David, Solomon, Esther, Isaiah, Jonah, John the Baptist, Mary, Peter, Thomas, Paul or Timothy. Compile a list of facts about the individual you are studying, such as:

1. Meeting with God, or conversion.
2. Call to service.
3. Strong points (such as faith, obedience, prayer life, trust and so on).
4. Weak points (sins, failures).
5. Accomplishments.
6. Influence.
7. Name (note changes in name and look up the meaning of the name).
8. Characteristics you should follow.
9. Characteristics you should avoid.
10. What God said about this person.

You may not be able to find all of these facts about each individual, but learn all that you can from what the Bible says about him or her.

You may want to study the Bible by the comparative method. This means that you will compare Scripture with Scripture. In other words, you will compare one passage of Scripture with what the

Bible says about the same (or similar) topics in other places in the Bible. The best commentary on the Bible is the Bible itself. When you are studying a certain portion or chapter of the Bible and find a difficult passage you do not understand, try to find another passage similar to it (or at least one dealing with the same subject) to help explain its meaning. The best aid in using this method, in addition to the marginal references found in many Bibles, is a book entitled *Treasury of Scripture Knowledge.* It lists several cross-references to every verse of the Bible. A great Bible teacher once said, "One will get more light on passages of Scripture by looking up the references given in the *Treasury of Scripture Knowledge* than in any other way I know."

Another way of studying the Bible is to use one of the Bible study courses available. You can find courses on a wide variety of topics, including studies on a particular subject, a book of the Bible or a Bible character. Your local Christian bookstore or your pastor could assist you in finding one of interest to you.

No matter what method you choose, your goal should be to grow in your understanding of what the Bible teaches. And when you know what it teaches, it's your responsibility to obey it.

Chapter 7

Your Testimony to Others

It is impossible to live the Christian life in secret, although some try to do so. The new life imparted to every believer when he accepts Christ as Saviour must manifest itself outwardly. The only way to live a successful Christian life is to live it openly, without shame or fear. Not only are we to be Christlike in our behavior, but we are also to talk about Christ openly.

Why must Christ be spoken of audibly? To begin with, the Lord Himself commanded us to confess Him publicly. He said, "Whosoever therefore shall confess me before men, him will I confess also before my Father which is in heaven" (Matt. 10:32). If we acknowledge our relationship with Him on earth, He will acknowledge His relationship with us before His Father in heaven. So it is actually for our sake that He requires this confession.

Romans 10:9,10, says, "If you confess with your mouth Jesus as Lord, and believe in your heart that God raised Him from the dead, you shall be saved; for with the heart man believes, resulting in righteousness, and with the mouth he confesses, resulting in salvation" (NASB). These verses show that what a person believes will naturally be apparent by what he says. Open confession will confirm the fact that he is saved. Therefore, audible confession of the Saviour is very important.

In the second place, we should confess Christ openly because it is a source of help and strength to us. Every time a Christian talks about Christ and his relationship with Him, he is strengthened spiritually. A witnessing Christian is not in much danger of habitually sinning, but failure to witness can be the beginning of backsliding. To testify of the Lord publicly will make you strong, and it is also a source of genuine joy. Many believers who tremble with timidity and fear as they attempt to give their testimony for Christ overflow with joy after their witness is given. Witnessing is a source of inner strength and satisfaction.

In addition, a clear confession of your faith often solves many problems. When unsaved people know that you are a Christian, they will often stop trying to urge you to participate in unchristian activities. Let people know right from the start where you stand. This will save you much embarrassment and grief. The world may not love a dedicated Christian, but it will usually respect him. On the other hand, wavering or hypocritical Christians aren't taken seriously and are constantly being coaxed to do things that even unbelievers recognize as violating Christian principles. Therefore, to speak out boldly for Christ can be a means of victory over temptation.

Doesn't it seem logical that you would want to

speak unashamedly about the Saviour who has done such great things for you? When a friend does a favor or is especially kind, are we reluctant to make it known? Don't we instead take every possible opportunity to tell people about it? Rather than being ashamed of such friends, we are proud of them. Shouldn't it be the same with the Friend who gave His life to save us? If a child has a faithful, loving father, is it natural for the child to be ashamed of him or reluctant to acknowledge him as his father? Aren't children usually proud of their fathers? Would a wife ever be ashamed to introduce her husband? If he is a good husband, she is happy and proud to introduce him to others and to talk about him. As Christians, we are called "the Bride of Christ" in the Bible. But are we ashamed of Christ or afraid to tell others about Him?

People who know that you are a Christian will expect you to act in a Christlike manner and to talk about your Saviour. If they detect that you are ashamed of your faith, they certainly will never respect you. They will consider your Christian faith weak and your Christian experience invalid. If you claim to be a believer yet are afraid to discuss your faith openly, you leave unbelievers puzzled. They will regard you as a hypocrite. They will certainly not want to consider such a faith for themselves.

So how should you begin to witness for Christ to others? If you have been hiding your Christianity from other believers, the first step you need to take is to publicly testify to them of your faith. Perhaps you attend a church that has a testimony time as

56

part of the regular church service. Perhaps your pastor gives an invitation during the service where those who want to can publicly acknowledge decisions they have made. Take advantage of these opportunities, or talk to your pastor about how to testify in your church of your faith.

Baptism is also an excellent way to testify of your faith before others. Baptism is primarily a public confession that we have experienced cleansing from our sins. The waters of baptism, which touch only the outer surface of our physical body, were never intended to wash away sin. Instead, the ceremony is a picture of our death to the old life and our "resurrection" to a new life in Christ; it is also symbolic of our cleansing by His blood (Heb. 9:14; Rev. 1:5). For a scriptural study of the true significance of baptism, examine Romans 6. According to the Scriptures, people are not baptized in order to be saved but as a testimony of the fact that they are saved.

The Lord commanded His followers to baptize all of those whom they made disciples (Matt. 28:19). In the early church, from its beginning at Pentecost, all who accepted Christ as Saviour were baptized. In this way they signified, or confessed, their identity with Jesus Christ and His followers.

Since baptism was commanded by Christ and was practiced by His first followers and since it is a public testimony to others that Christ is our Saviour, it is very important. It is not a matter of personal choice but of divine injunction. Thus, every believer, including those who may have been baptized before they were saved, should be baptized as a believer.

Church membership should logically follow baptism, but that will be discussed in chapter 11.

It is not enough to publicly confess Christ only once. Never be ashamed to speak for Him and to let people know you belong to Him, both in private life and in public testimony meetings. At church, at home, at work, at school, at play—always let people know where you stand. Of course, your testimony must always be humble. Any degree of pride will make your witness ineffective.

Confess Christ faithfully to your relatives and closest friends. How can you expect to live a true Christian life if you don't let those closest to you know that you now belong to Christ? Let them hear of Him in your conversation and see Him in your life. If you fail here, among those closest to you, you will not be strong in the Lord elsewhere. Some may be offended, but others may trust the Saviour as a result of your testimony.

Speak of Christ clearly before your acquaintances and associates. Never be afraid or ashamed. Make Him known to all with whom you come in contact. Let them know that you love and serve Christ. Never let it be said by anyone you know, either in this life or in eternity, "He never told me about Jesus!"

Jesus plainly told His disciples that they were to be His witnesses (Luke 24:48; Acts 1:8). They regarded themselves as such and faithfully filled that role (Acts 5:29-39; 10:39). This title is actually a legal term. What is a witness? It is one who knows something. No one will ever be called to the witness stand who does not know something about the case being tried. That person must have seen, heard, felt, tasted or smelled something that will provide evidence. A witness cannot give opinions or deductions. He must relate what he knows to be the facts through his own senses, through personal experience and contact. To be a witness for Christ, you must know something about Him through personal contact.

You must know by personal experience that you have been saved before you can effectively tell anyone else that Jesus saves. You must have assurance of your salvation. Remember, the testimony of any witness may be cross-examined by some tough questions from others. Can you testify that Jesus saves because you know you are saved? Is your knowledge of His salvation personal, positive and real? If your testimony is uncertain or indefinite, it will not convince others.

You must know by personal experience that God answers prayer. Can you give some specific examples of how He has answered some of your personal petitions—examples that no one can contradict? Unless you can, how will you be able to convince others that God cares for His children? If you say that your pastor says so or that the church believes it, you will never convince your friends that the Lord hears and answers prayer. But if you can share some personal experiences, others may have a

59

desire to become acquainted with this caring God.

You must know by experience that Christ can satisfy all the inner longings of the human heart before you can testify to that fact. Other people may not believe the beautiful phrases in the hymnal. They may not even accept the promises in the Bible. But it will be hard for them to refute the fact if you can tell or show them how Christ has met your needs. Can you tell them how He gave you peace and joy during very stressful circumstances? Can you tell them how He gave you love for your spouse when that person was very unlovable? People are searching for that kind of God and will listen to what you say about Him.

You must know personally that Christ gives victory over sin. Has He given you some definite victories over habitual sins, and are you enjoying such victory now? When you try to introduce someone to Christ, they may say, "I'm afraid I couldn't keep from sinning." They need to know that Christ gives a believer power over sin. They also need to know that no Christian is perfect and that when we do sin, the Lord will forgive and cleanse us if we confess the sin to Him. Such a testimony will be far more effective than a sermon preached from a pulpit.

A witness must be willing to tell what he knows. A person who will not testify, no matter how well he knows the facts or how important those facts are to the future of others, cannot be a witness. A witness must be willing to declare what he knows and to answer any questions. For a witness to remain silent is tragic. Imagine a person's remaining silent while someone is being condemned to death when what he knows could set that person free!

Ezekiel 33:8 says, "When I say unto the wicked, O wicked man, thou shalt surely die; if thou dost not speak to warn the wicked from his way, that wicked man shall die in his iniquity; but his blood will I require at thine hand." This is a solemn warning. As witnesses of God's saving grace to lost sinners, we dare not remain silent. We must share what we know. Every Christian should speak boldly to tell others what he has come to know about Jesus Christ in his own life.

The testimony of a witness can be affected by his behavior. His words must be supported by his life. Otherwise, what he says will be disregarded. The personal character of any court witness largely determines the value of his testimony to the judge or jury. If the witness is known to be unreliable, what he shares will not be taken seriously. But if this person is known for integrity and honesty, his words will have tremendous impact. Defense lawyers watch for every opportunity to point out flaws in the character of a witness and thus undermine his testimony. So it is with the Christian; unbelievers watch closely for any inconsistencies between what we say and what we do. Our lives must conform to our words. We cannot profess one thing and do another if people are to believe what we say.

Strive to keep your behavior above reproach. When you do sin, go to Christ immediately for forgiveness and cleansing. If you offend another person, go to him, apologize and ask his forgiveness. If you practice this, people will respect you and your testimony. Read Acts 4:13; Titus 2:7,8; I Peter 2:11,12,15; 3:15,16. If these verses describe your life, your testimony will be effective.

A true witness never retracts what he says. Since what he shares is the truth, he stands by it. He will never alter or compromise his words. The Greek word translated "witness" in the New Testament is the word from which we also get the word "martyr." A true witness is willing to die for what he believes.

Many Christians have died because of their testimony for Christ. Some of them suffered immensely; but they did not retract their words or their faith, and they died trusting Christ. Believers in many lands today still suffer and die because of their witness. We should also be ready to suffer or even to die for what we believe, though we may not have to do so. When we remember how much Christ endured for us, no amount of suffering should be too great to face because of our love for Him. Let us be faithful witnesses, just as He was once a faithful witness for us on earth—and still is at the right hand of the throne of God (see Rev. 1:5).

Chapter 8

Your Responsibility

Second Corinthians 5:15,18,20 says, "He [Christ] died for all, that they which live should not henceforth live unto themselves, but unto him which died for them, and rose again. . . . And all things are of God, who hath reconciled us to himself by Jesus Christ, and hath given to us the ministry of reconciliation. . . . Now then we are ambassadors for Christ, as though God did beseech you by us: we pray you in Christ's stead, be ye reconciled to God."

According to these verses, Christians are to be Christ's representatives, telling others how to be reconciled to God. This ministry has been committed to us. Only as we share with others the Gospel of the grace of the Lord Jesus Christ will they ever be saved. This is our responsibility, our task, here on earth.

An ambassador is one who has been selected to be the authorized representative or messenger of another. Every Christian has been appointed an ambassador for Christ. We are to represent Christ to others and urge them to be reconciled to God through Him. We must be faithful to fulfill this responsibility.

This is exactly what Andrew did, and a beautiful tribute is paid to him in John 1:41. After he had found Jesus as his Messiah and Saviour, "he first findeth his own brother Simon, and saith unto him, We have found the Messias." As soon as Andrew became a follower of Christ, he had a desire to bring others to Him, and he began by bringing his own brother to the Lord. His brother, Peter, later became a strong leader in the early church. This should be an encouragement to us. You might think you can accomplish very little for the Lord, yet you might introduce someone to Christ who will reach thousands for the Lord. The person who led D. L. Moody to Christ had no idea that Moody would bring thousands to the Saviour.

If you want to be a real Christian, follow Andrew's example. Try to win others to Christ, and begin with your own family. Notice how simple Andrew's testimony was. He simply said, "We have found the Messiah." You could begin by telling your friends and relatives, "I have found the Saviour." We do not know what God will use to save others. He may use a simple testimony of our salvation experience, just as Andrew's testimony resulted in Simon Peter's salvation.

The Apostle Paul said, "And He [Christ] gave some as apostles, and some as prophets, and some as evangelists, and some as pastors and teachers, for the equipping of the saints for the work of service, to the building up of the body of Christ; until we all attain to the unity of the faith, and of the knowledge of the Son of God, to a mature man, to the measure of the stature which belongs to the fulness of Christ" (Eph. 4:11-13, NASB). Notice that the Head of the Church, Jesus Christ, has given some gift, or special ability, to every Christian. Every one of us has some part in "the work of service." He has also appointed some to train and equip us for that service.

Notice that the ultimate aim of this service is to build up Christ's Body, the Church. As Christians all over the world engage in the task of bringing others to Christ, His Body will ultimately be built up, or completed. At the proper point in God's eternal timetable, Christ will return to take His children home to be with Him (I Thess. 4:16,17). The joyous prospect that "we shall always be with the Lord" (v. 17, NASB) is a powerful incentive to share the Gospel with as many as possible.

In the last chapter, we saw how important it is to openly share with others what Christ means to us. One of the primary reasons for doing this is to create a desire in others to know the Lord in a personal way too.

We are not to live for ourselves, for our own personal pleasures and pursuits. We are to live for Christ (see II Cor. 5:15). And the life that is most pleasing to Christ is the life dedicated to winning others to Him. When He told His disciples that they were to be His witnesses throughout the world (Acts 1:8), the main objective of that witness was to bring men and women to Jesus Christ from "every kindred, and tongue, and people, and nation" (Rev. 5:9).

When you came to Christ, no doubt the primary objective of your coming was to save yourself. But now that you are saved, your objective should be to help save others. No other goal is suitable for you as a Christian or pleases your Lord. The reason why Christ is so eager to have us confess Him before men is so that, through our confession, they might come to know Him as their Saviour.

If the Lord did not have such a purpose for leaving us here on earth, it would be better for Him to take us home to heaven as soon as we are saved. That would save us much heartache, and it would also save Him much grief. But He has a purpose for leaving us here. He wants us to shine as lights before others so that those who are now in darkness can come to know Him as their God and Saviour (see Matt. 5:14-16; Phil. 2:15). If you are a young Christian, God has great plans for your life; and if He allows you to live a long time, it will be only for this purpose—that many may hear the Gospel through you. If you are older and have known the Lord for a long time, His reason for sparing your life thus far is to allow you to be His witness. Has that purpose been realized in your life, or have you disappointed your Saviour?

John 15 records our Lord's beautiful illustration of our relationship to Him—that of the vine and the branches. John 15:5 says, "I am the vine, ye are the branches: He that abideth in me, and I in him, the same bringeth forth much fruit: for without me ye can do nothing."

The Lord was pointing out through this figure His

indispensability to us. As the vine is indispensable to the branch, so Christ is indispensable to His people. He said, "Without me ye can do nothing." As the branch cannot live or bear fruit apart from the vine, neither can we apart from Christ. He is indispensable to our salvation as well as to our spiritual life and health and fruitfulness. We have no strength apart from Him. It is easy to see this truth in His illustration.

But another truth is also taught very subtly in this same illustration. It is that the branch is indispensable to the vine. Just as the branch cannot bear fruit without the vine, neither can the vine bear fruit without the branch. Fruit is always produced on the branches of the tree, never on the vine, or trunk. This is God's order both in nature and in the spiritual realm. Remember that Christ said, "Ye are the branches" (v. 5). That means we are also indispensable to Him. He has chosen to produce fruit through us. We are His witnesses, and only as we share the Gospel with others will they come to know the Saviour. We are His instruments.

Aside from what people can learn about God through nature and His Word, His only witness since the time of Pentecost is His people. He works through us to reveal Himself to others. The Holy Spirit indwells us and works through us. As Christians pray, witness, preach, talk about the Saviour and live a Christlike life, people will be saved.

God has chosen to use us to accomplish His work. He could have used angels or spoken to each person audibly, but He has chosen to work through humans who will depend on Him. If we do not tell others about Christ, how will they hear? If we do not use our feet to go to other countries to share the Gospel, who will? If we do not use our minds and abilities to learn other languages and translate the Scriptures into those languages, how will those people know of God's love or of Christ's saving grace and atoning death on Calvary's cross? The only witness He has among humans of His mercy and grace is our witness (see Rom. 10:13-15). How can we fail Him?

You may find it difficult at first to share God's message with another person. But once you have seen someone trust Christ as a result of your witness, you will never want to stop. The evangelist D. L. Moody determined never to let one day pass without speaking to someone about salvation and trying to bring that one to Christ. Don't think that you have to be eloquent or clever to tell others what you know about Christ—just share what He has done for you.

Often the greatest problem in witnessing is how to start the conversation. Carry some good Gospel tracts with you, and pass them out whenever the opportunity arises. They will often open the way for a conversation about spiritual topics. Then you can tell the person how you were saved and how he can be saved, too, by trusting Christ.

Another way to start a conversation is to wear a small pin on your lapel or collar. This will attract the attention of people and cause them to ask questions. I once wore a gold question mark on the lapel of my coat. When people asked me about it, I would ask them, "Well, what is the most important question in the world?" Then I would go on to say that I considered "Have you accepted Christ as your Saviour?" to be the most important question in life.

A friend of mine wore the number "3" on his lapel. Whenever people asked him what it stood for, he would tell them, "The Trinity—the Father, the Son and the Holy Spirit." Then he would go on to explain how God the Father loved mankind, how Christ—His Son—died for us and how the Holy Spirit wanted to come into the heart and transform the life of anyone who would accept the Saviour.

R. A. Torrey, Jr., once related the great joy he experienced when he saw his first person come to Christ. While the invitation was being given, during a meeting in which his father was preaching, young Torrey asked the first young man he saw if he would like to come to Christ. To his amazement, the young man responded by immediately going to the altar. Young Torrey then led that young man to Christ. He later testified that it was the greatest experience in his spiritual life since his own salvation. It can be your experience too. Once you see one person trust Christ, it will be the joy and desire of your life to win others to the Saviour.

The most convincing part of your testimony to others will be a genuine love for them. People almost always respond to love, and when they see that you really do care about them, they will not be angry when you try to talk to them about Christ. If you speak to them in love, they may see their need of becoming acquainted with your Saviour. If you find you don't have this love for others, ask the Lord to fill you with His love, for this is one of the ministries of the Holy Spirit (Rom. 5:5). Any effort to witness to a person that stems from genuine love, even though it may be done poorly, will not fail to have an impact on that person and may even result in his salvation.

We cannot overemphasize the value of prayer in witnessing either. If we begin the task without praying that God will use us and enable us to communicate His message and love effectively, our efforts will fail. But if we ask Him for power, grace and love in our lives and then go out with a sincere desire to bring our friends and acquaintances to the Saviour, our efforts will be abundantly rewarded.

If you want to be a real Christian, fulfill your responsibility to be Christ's ambassador. Begin by praying, and then speak to the first person you meet who needs your Saviour.

Chapter 9

Your Relationship to the World

Perhaps the greatest test in the Christian's life comes in his relationship to the world. Some Christians find it hard to let go of certain worldly attractions that hinder their spiritual growth and progress.

When I was young, I remember going into a restaurant that had a machine for testing how much electrical current you could stand. The machine had a pair of "hot" grips, and the closer you drew them together, the stronger the current became. A dial indicated how much current you were getting. The idea, of course, was to outdo the other fellow. After several of my companions had taken hold of the grips, drawn them slowly together and let go again, I stepped up to the machine. I had decided that instead of drawing the handles together slowly, I would just force them together with one big push. I did this, but to my amazement, the current became so strong that I was unable to let go! What an experience that was! The electricity shot through my body and hurt me, but I was unable to let go.

That is exactly the way it seems with many attractions of the world. While the person clinging to them knows he is being hurt, he doesn't seem to be able to let go. No honest person can deny the magnetic attraction of the world. Each one of us finds that the world appeals to certain areas of our lives.

Various passages of Scripture speak of the Christian's relationship to the world. Jesus told the disciples, "Ye are not of the world" (John 15:19). Paul told us in Titus 2:12 how we should live after salvation: "Teaching us that, denying ungodliness and worldly lusts, we should live soberly, righteously, and godly, in this present world."

In Ephesians 2, the same apostle pointed out the contrast that should be evident in our behavior after salvation. In verses 2 and 3 he spoke of our lives prior to conversion: "Wherein in time past ye walked according to the course of this world, according to the prince of the power of the air, the spirit that now worketh in the children of disobedience: among whom also we all had our conversation in times past [formerly lived] in the lusts of our flesh, fulfilling the desires of the flesh and of the mind; and were by nature the children of wrath." In verses 12 and 13 he showed the contrast: "That at that time ye were without Christ . . . and without God in the world: but now in Christ Jesus ye who sometimes were far off are made nigh by the blood of Christ." Before we were saved, we followed the course of this world, the desires of Satan and the lusts of the flesh; but coming to know Christ gives us a new power to resist the former temptations.

In II Timothy 4:10 the apostle wrote: "For Demas hath forsaken me, having loved this present world."

It is apparent that believers can sometimes fall back into their old habits and desires because their love for the world is stronger than their love for Christ.

In James 4:4 we find this strong statement: "Ye adulterers and adulteresses, know ye not that the friendship of the world is enmity with God? whosoever therefore will be a friend of the world is the enemy of God." And in I John 2:15 notice these words: "Love not the world, neither the things that are in the world. If any man love the world, the love of the Father is not in him." A command is given in II Corinthians 6:17, warning against partnership with an unbeliever: "Wherefore come out from among them, and be ye separate, saith the Lord, and touch not the unclean thing; and I will receive you."

A true Christian must hear and obey what the Word of God says about his relationship to this sinful world. When a person has trusted Christ and experienced a transformation in his life, he will want to give up many habits and pleasures that are not compatible with his new life in Christ. First John 5:19 says, "The whole world lieth in wickedness." This is why we must be careful of our association with the world and what it offers. Anyone who looks at the world system objectively can see that, on the whole, it has departed far from God and is full of all kinds of evil. At best the world is indifferent to God, Jesus Christ and anything spiritual; at worst it demonstrates outright hatred. The world is controlled by Satan and therefore is centered around what is unholy and evil. Most of the world's pleasures and entertainments appeal to the lust of the flesh or the lust of the eyes or are harmful to the body.

Christians should realize that they cannot agree with the standards of the world. When you believe in the Lord Jesus Christ and follow Him, you immediately face some pertinent questions that demand clear-cut answers. You must decide how you will spend your leisure time and who you will spend it with. Enough has been written and said regarding specific practices to make long discussions unnecessary.

Any honest person must acknowledge that much of the world's entertainment glorifies crime, infidelity and lust and is generated by a desire to make money. Many of these "pleasures" adversely affect the mind and can even be harmful to the body.

Any habit that controls a person and that has ill effects on his or her physical or mental well-being certainly is not proper for a child of God. It will prove to be a detriment to the human body and a hindrance to that individual's Christian testimony. Our bodies are temples of the Holy Spirit (I Cor. 3:16), and we are responsible to care for them in a way that glorifies God. If we proclaim to the world a Christ who is able to give them victory over their sins and evil habits and yet are ourselves enslaved by some practice, our testimony will most certainly be weakened.

Do not get the impression that the Christian life is dull. When the Scriptures refer to separation, it almost always has two aspects—not only a separation "from" but also a separation "to." We are separated *from* the world *to* God. When the Lord asks us to give up something, He gives us something much better to replace it.

The more we dedicate ourselves to serving Christ and the better we know Him, the less appeal the world and its attractions will have for us. We will automatically separate ourselves from those things. On the last night Jesus was with His disciples before His crucifixion, He pointed out to them that they were *in* the world but not *of* the world (John 15:19; 17:15,16). This is exactly our position as Christians. He has chosen us from among the people of the world and separated us to Himself as His own peculiar people. The Church—made up of believers— has been called out and separated from the world. Therefore, we should live in such a way that others will see a difference in us.

If we imitate the world and pattern our lives after its standards, how will people know that we are Christ's disciples? But if they see a difference between our lives and their lives, they will want to know why. Then we will have an opportunity to tell them about our personal relationship with Christ.

Is the price too great to pay? God has left us in this world to guide others to Him. So we should not seclude ourselves or withdraw from the people of the world, but we should live like children of God in a world filled with wickedness.

After all, the world is a very empty and unsatisfying place. The Book of Ecclesiastes relates how Solomon tried everything the world could offer but found no satisfaction or peace in it. He came to the conclusion that it was all "vanity" (1:2). In his quest for fulfillment, Solomon tried education and wisdom, thinking that human knowledge would satisfy the thirst of his inner being (1:13-18). But he concluded that it was all "vexation of spirit" and "vanity."

He then turned to pleasure, indulging fully in all of the amusements of the world (2:1-11). But this he found was also vanity. He also tried to satisfy his longings with the wealth of the world. He secured everything that money could buy, thinking that this would surely bring him satisfaction (2:4-11). But his conclusion was that all was "vanity and vexation of spirit."

If any man was ever in a position to completely test the world, Solomon was. And if the world's knowledge and pleasures and wealth could not bring satisfaction to a great man like Solomon, it surely cannot do so for any of us. Those who have experienced all that the world has to offer will come to the same conclusion Solomon did—that it is all empty and void. "For what shall it profit a man, if he shall gain the whole world, and lose his own soul?" (Mark 8:36).

The pleasures of the world have a strong appeal and promise satisfaction, but they are disillusioning and deceitful. The world cannot keep its promises. It leaves people unsatisfied, unfulfilled and empty. Often those who have acquired a large amount of wealth or experienced all of the world's pleasures are the ones who commit suicide. Why, then, would the Christian become attached to such an empty and false world?

Instead, the Christian should "seek those things which are above, where Christ sitteth on the right hand of God" (Col. 3:1). You should "set your affection on things above, not on things on the earth" (v. 2), "for where your treasure is, there will your heart be also" (Matt. 6:21). Where is your treasure? Where are your affections? The Apostle John said, "Love not the world, neither the things that are in the world. If any man love the world, the love of the Father is not in him" (I John 2:15). If we love God, we cannot love the world at the same time. If our relationship to Christ is right, our relationship to the world is clear—we won't be attracted to its empty promises.

In trying to decide whether a certain activity is right or wrong for you as a Christian, it will help to have some general principles to follow. Try asking yourself these questions:

1. Will it displease Christ or break my fellowship with Him?
2. Will it dishonor God?
3. Would it be something Jesus would not do?
4. Will it damage my testimony to others?
5. Will it hinder my spiritual growth and maturity?

If the answer to any of these questions is yes, then it would not be right for you to pursue this activity.

Remember that what is right for one Christian may be entirely wrong for another. Some believers can go certain places, do certain things and win others to Christ in the process; whereas other believers will sin and be a stumbling block to others in the same situation. So for that reason, always apply these five test questions to anything about which you are in doubt. Almost every question or problem regarding your relationship to the world can then be settled.

God says to us, "Whatsoever ye do, do it heartily, as to the Lord, and not unto men; knowing that of the Lord ye shall receive the reward of the inheritance: for ye serve the Lord Christ" (Col. 3:23,24). In verse 17 we read a stronger statement: "And whatsoever ye do in word or deed, do all in the name of the Lord Jesus, giving thanks to God and the Father by him." This is similar to what Paul wrote in I Corinthians 10:31,32: "Whether therefore ye eat, or drink, or whatsoever ye do, do all to the glory of God. Give none offence, neither to the Jews, nor to the Gentiles, nor to the church of God."

If you can't go to a certain place in the name of Christ, to the glory of God and without harming your testimony, don't go. If you can't participate in a certain activity without compromising your beliefs or offending someone, don't participate. If you can't do something without being ashamed of it or without harming your body, don't do it. Ask yourself, *Would Christ be pleased, or would I be ashamed for Him to see me?*

As Christians, we should not try to see how close we can come to the fire without being burned but how far we can stay from danger. If we are in doubt about something we want to do, it is best not to do it. We would not want to do anything that would cause others to stumble and prevent them from coming to Christ.

Chapter 10

Your Inner Helper

The preceding chapters have presented some of the great challenges and responsibilities of the Christian life. Perhaps you have been tempted to think that all of this is too difficult for you and that you can never live that kind of a Christian life. Perhaps you feel you can never be a real Christian.

If it were up to us alone to attain these goals, it would be impossible. In our own human strength we could never live such Christian lives. But we are not left to our own strength and resources. We have a very competent inner helper, a personal enabler — the Holy Spirit.

The Lord Jesus, before His ascension, repeatedly promised His disciples that the Holy Spirit would come to abide in them and to strengthen them. He said, "I will pray the Father, and he shall give you another Comforter, that he may abide with you for ever; even the Spirit of truth" (John 14:16,17). He also told them, "When the Comforter is come, whom I will send unto you from the Father, even the Spirit of truth, which proceedeth from the Father, he shall testify of me: and ye also shall bear witness" (15:26,27). The disciples did not understand why Jesus had to go away, but He told them,

"It is expedient for you that I go away: for if I go not away, the Comforter will not come unto you; but if I depart, I will send him unto you" (16:7).

The Holy Spirit was sent to indwell every believer. In I Corinthians 3:16 Paul wrote to the believers: "Know ye not that ye are the temple of God, and that the Spirit of God dwelleth in you?" In the same book he also asked, "What? know ye not that your body is the temple of the Holy Ghost which is in you, which ye have of God, and ye are not your own?" (6:19). The Apostle Paul confidently prayed that the Ephesian believers would be "strengthened with might by his Spirit in the inner man" (Eph. 3:16) so that they would attain spiritual maturity in the Christian life.

The Holy Spirit is our inner helper, and by His power and strength we are able to meet all the challenges that come to us as Christians and to live a victorious Christian life. What is impossible in our strength is possible through His power. Christ's words in John 14:18 about the coming of the Holy Spirit literally mean, "I will not leave you orphans." Without the Holy Spirit to help us meet our enemies and assume our responsibilities, we would be like helpless, orphaned children. The Lord Jesus knew this very well. Therefore, as He said farewell to His disciples, He promised to send the Holy Spirit to dwell in them and to strengthen them for their Christian life and service.

The promise of the Holy Spirit's indwelling is the heritage of every Christian. When a person is born again, he is "born . . . of the Spirit" (3:5). In other

81

words, at the moment a person is saved, the Holy Spirit comes into his soul and implants the life of God in him. Then he can rely on Him for the strength and power he needs to live a life pleasing to God. Even the weakest Christian can have courage when he remembers that the Holy Spirit is there to overcome his weaknesses through His divine power.

We see in the Bible that the Holy Spirit can help us in a variety of ways. First, He helps us understand the Bible (John 16:12-14). Understanding of the Bible comes, not through human intellect but by divine enlightenment. It is the mission of the Holy Spirit to guide God's people into divine truth. So when you read the Bible, read it prayerfully. When you come to passages you don't understand, ask the Lord to show you the correct interpretation. He is the author of the Scriptures (II Pet. 1:20,21), and He is its best interpreter.

The second way the Holy Spirit helps us is by placing God's love in our hearts (Rom. 5:5). Love is our most vital need—love for God, love for fellow Christians and love for all people. The first and greatest commandment of the Old Testament was that people should love the Lord their God with all their heart. And the second commandment was to love their neighbor as themselves (see Matt. 22:35-39). The emphasis of the New Testament is the same. After Peter had denied Jesus, the Lord's question to him was simply "Do you love Me?" (see John 21:15-17). He also gave His disciples a "new" commandment: "A new commandment I give unto you, That ye love one another; . . . by this shall all men know that ye are my disciples, if ye have love one to another" (13:34,35). One of the greatest needs in our world today is the need for love between Christians. This love is seriously lacking and is a stumbling block to unbelievers. Unless those around us see the love of Christ demonstrated in our lives, how will we ever win them to Christ?

Love is unquestionably our greatest need. If you want to learn more about showing Christian love, study the First Epistle of John. We cannot force ourselves to feel loving toward someone we don't like, but the Holy Spirit can fill us with God's love for that person if we let Him do it. So when we are conscious of a coldness and a lack of love in our hearts, we should ask the Lord to give us the will to love in spite of our feelings. As we allow the Lord to work in our lives and we are filled with the Holy Spirit, we will be filled with the love of God.

A third area in which the Holy Spirit helps us is by giving us strength against sin. Christ freed us from the penalty of sin, and the Holy Spirit gives us power over sin. We call this sanctification. "Such [unrighteous people] were some of you: but ye are washed, but ye are sanctified . . . by the Spirit of our God" (I Cor. 6:11). When we allow the Holy Spirit to help us, we will no longer be enslaved by our sinful desires. "Walk in the Spirit, and ye shall not fulfil the lust of the flesh" (Gal. 5:16). The inner strength that He supplies will enable us to be victorious over sin and over Satan. So when you feel yourself being tempted to sin, breathe a prayer then and there, and the Holy Spirit will not fail to give you the strength you need.

Fourth, the Holy Spirit aids us in prayer (Rom. 8:26,27). He is the One, first of all, who urges us to pray. The Spirit frequently prompts us to pray by bringing a certain situation or person to mind. At such times we should cooperate with the Spirit and follow His leading. The Holy Spirit also teaches us how to pray and reminds us what to pray for. Often we do not know how to pray, but the Holy Spirit intercedes for us with groanings too deep for words. Christ intercedes for us in heaven before the Father on the throne, while the Holy Spirit intercedes for us on earth.

By ourselves, we would often ask for what seems good or pleasant to us but what would be far from best for us. But the Holy Spirit knows what is best for us, and He prompts us to ask for those things. He comes to our aid. He produces the right desires within us.

Prayer is not merely asking God to grant our natural desires, nor is it merely beautiful words. Real prayer occurs when the Holy Spirit produces holy desires within us and then intensifies them to such an extent that we will not rest or stop praying until God has answered that petition.

Satan attacks our prayer life more than anything else, so we need a helper. The Holy Spirit gives us the desire to pray and enables us to pray. When you find yourself unable to pray, depend on the Holy Spirit to come to your rescue. It is one of His ministries to you, and He loves to perform it.

Fifth, the Holy Spirit directs and leads in the lives of God's people (Rom. 8:14). Often we do not know what to do and cannot determine the will of God. At such times the Holy Spirit is there to lead and guide us. In the morning, before you face your daily tasks, earnestly ask the Lord to guide every thought, every word, every decision during that day. Then, throughout the day, as you face problems, needs and dilemmas, pray for specific guidance. The Holy Spirit has come to be your Guide, and He can help you know what to do.

The Holy Spirit helps us in a sixth way. He produces spiritual fruit in the Christian's life (Gal. 5:22,23). The Holy Spirit wants to fill believers with love and joy, give them peace and make them patient. He imparts and increases their faith. The Holy Spirit can also give believers the ability to be meek and self-controlled, restraining their natural appetites and desires. As we walk in obedience to the Lord, we will find the Holy Spirit producing His fruit in our lives. All the blessings of the Christian life are imparted and ministered to us by the Holy Spirit.

Many Christians are not aware of the presence of the Holy Spirit. That is a tragedy. The Holy Spirit is a person as much as God the Father or Jesus Christ is. And He indwells every Christian. If you will give Him complete control of your life, He will lead you into the abundant life.

Learn to cultivate fellowship with the Holy Spirit. Think of Him as an indwelling presence, a real person. Contemplate His desire for your growth and spiritual prosperity. Consider His goodness, His graciousness and His willingness to help you at all times. Learn to rely on Him for all of your spiritual needs. Learn to talk to Him and to commune with Him. Learn to draw from Him all the spiritual qualities that He wants to manifest in your life. Think of Him as He really is—a heavenly guest, the lover of your soul. He is your friend, your companion, your comforter, your guide, your helper, your teacher. Let Him be your all in all.

Chapter 11

Your Worship

Jesus said to the woman of Samaria, "God is a Spirit: and they that worship him must worship him in spirit and in truth" (John 4:24). For believers, worshiping God is primarily a spiritual exercise— that is, we worship Him in our hearts. We should be worshiping and praising the Lord all day long, but that doesn't eliminate the need for special times set aside for the purpose of worship—times when all other activity ceases.

The believer's personal prayer life has already been discussed, so this chapter will consider the worship of God in our homes and in the church.

Almost nothing can be of greater value in any home than family worship. We sometimes refer to this as the "family altar." It is a time set apart every day when the whole family can worship the Lord through reading the Bible and praying together. Nothing will do more to instill the fear of God and the love of God in the hearts of children, and nothing will so help to eliminate family differences and troubles than a time of family worship. When the family meets together for prayer and worship, hard feelings and unkind thoughts can be resolved.

No husband and wife can pray together daily without being in true harmony with each other. When differences do arise, they will either stop praying or else be quickly reconciled.

The family altar is indispensable to the home. No greater heritage can be left to the children of Christian parents than the memory of studying God's Word and praying together as a family.

Now that you have become a Christian, begin family worship in your home. Set aside a time for it each day. Perhaps right after breakfast or after supper will be the best time. Begin by going through a book of the Bible, reading a chapter or a short section each time. Then pray together, with as many participating as possible. Some days there may only be time for the father or mother to pray, but you should plan for times when the children can also pray. Every child who is old enough should be encouraged to participate. You should also take enough time for family worship so that questions the children have about the Bible text can be discussed. At times, the children should be given an opportunity to ask any questions they want to of the parents.

If you have small children in the home, it would be good to read frequently from a Bible story book and to give a few simple explanations of the story. If it is possible to have family worship twice a day, it may be helpful to use a good devotional book for one of the periods. Above all, the Bible should be read regularly.

Normally, the family altar should be led by the

father, since he is the head of the household. But circumstances may make it necessary for others to lead at times. If the husband is not a Christian but is willing for the wife to conduct family worship, then she should do so. The older children might even take turns leading the worship time.

Although it is often difficult to find time for the family altar, the dividends are infinitely worthwhile. The problem, of course, is infinitely greater in the home with an unsaved husband. But if he is willing for another member of the family to conduct family worship, then do so. If he is opposed to family worship and will not tolerate it, you need to pray for his salvation. God works wonders in answer to earnest prayer.

No matter what the odds are or how hard it may be to maintain the family altar, try to do so at any cost. During family worship, timid children can learn to pray aloud. Burdens can be freely shared with the Lord without fear or embarrassment. Teaching your family what the Bible says and helping them learn scriptural principles is essential. It should be your highest priority as a parent.

Now let's think about our worship together as a church family. Church membership is not essential to salvation, nor is it a part of salvation. But it is a definite part of the Christian life, and every believer should unite with some local church. The universal Church is a spiritual body, the Body of Christ, and every Christian is a member of that great organism. But the universal Church is made up of thousands of local congregations and assemblies all over the world. Every Christian should unite and fellowship with a local church for spiritual growth and help.

You may wonder which church you should join? Dr. R. A. Torrey once gave these guidelines:

1) Unite with a church that believes the Bible and preaches the Bible. Avoid a church that would tend to undermine your faith in the Bible as a reliable revelation from God Himself, the all-sufficient rule of faith and practice.

2) Unite with a church that believes in the power of prayer.

3) Unite with a church that has a genuine, active interest in the salvation of the lost, where young Christians are nurtured and helped, where both minister and people have a love for the poor and outcast.

4) Unite with a denomination whose doctrine, form of government and observance of the ordinances agree most closely with your own beliefs. But it is better to unite with a living church of some other denomination than to unite with a dead church of your own. We live in a day when denominational differences are becoming less and less important. The practices that divide the denominations are insignificant compared to the fundamental truths and purposes and faith that unite them.

5) If you cannot find a church that meets these criteria, find one that comes nearest to it. Look for what is good in the church and the pastor and do your best to strengthen it. Stand aloof, firmly but unobtrusively, from what is wrong and seek to correct it. Do not be discouraged if you cannot correct

it in a day, a week, a month or even a year. Patient love and prayer and effort will be effective in time. But do not criticize the church or the pastor. That will simply make you and the truths for which you stand repulsive.

Those are some very helpful guidelines in choosing a church. You may also want to ask yourself these questions concerning any church you may contemplate joining:

1. Does this church believe and proclaim the Bible to be the true Word of God and uphold it as such in all of the services?

2. Does the pastor preach clearly and simply about the atoning death of Christ on the cross and redemption through His shed blood?

3. Does this church emphasize that a person must experience the new birth through personal faith in Christ to be saved?

4. Is it a praying church? Are regular prayer meetings held in which the people participate?

5. Does it have a vital interest in foreign and home missions and have an active missionary program? Are missionaries supported and prayed for regularly? Are young people in the church being challenged to consider missionary service?

6. Are believers urged to witness for Christ and taught how to do it?

7. Is the literal, personal return of Jesus Christ to the earth believed and proclaimed?

If all of these questions can be answered yes, that church would be an excellent one to join. If they cannot all be answered yes, make sure that at least the first four can be. Do not join a church unless it believes in the inspiration of the Bible, the necessity of the shed blood of Christ, the new birth and true prayer.

Of course, it is not enough merely to join a church. You must attend regularly. Do not get into the habit of attending church sporadically. Make a real effort to be there at least for the Sunday services, including Sunday school, and the midweek service. Attend other services and activities as time and circumstances permit.

If you begin to neglect church attendance, you forfeit the fellowship you can enjoy there and you may begin to backslide in your Christian life. God, realizing how much we need Christian fellowship, has urged us not to forsake "the assembling of ourselves together" (Heb. 10:25). You need the encouragement and inspiration that comes from fellowship with the other Christians in your church, so be regular in your attendance.

If you, as a Christian, are unfaithful in your attendance, it will be a bad testimony to your unsaved friends and neighbors. They will expect you to go and will conclude that Christ doesn't mean very much to you if you don't attend. If you invite them to go to church with you to hear the Gospel, how can you expect them to do so if you are careless about your own attendance?

Not only should you join and regularly attend a church, but you should also participate in its activities and assume your share of its responsibilities. If you are asked to fill an office in the church, to teach a Sunday school class, to serve on a committee or perform some other duty, do so willingly as service to the Lord. Do the very best job you can with the help of the Holy Spirit. Decline only when you conscientiously feel that you are unqualified or unable to accept the position for some other reason. Even then, pray about it before refusing.

Of course, financial responsibilities accompany church membership, and you should expect to assume your part in those too. The expenses of operating a church can be met only as the members give. So give liberally and cheerfully to your church, as to the Lord. Giving will be discussed further in the next chapter.

The church is the believer's spiritual home while he is on earth. He should be encouraged, comforted and prepared for heaven there. He should enjoy fellowship with his spiritual family and share his prayer burdens with them. He should be able to turn to his church for spiritual help in times of need and perhaps for material help in some circumstances. He will be instructed in the Word of God and built up in the faith.

Every Christian needs the fellowship of other believers. The outward expression of this fellowship should be membership in a local church. If you avoid all organized churches, hoping to have a broader fellowship with all believers, you will only deceive yourself. You will miss the benefits that come from intimate union with a local congregation. If you have trusted the Lord Jesus Christ as your

Saviour, you will want to unite with a good church as soon as possible.

Remember that you will not find a perfect church. If you wait until you find a perfect church before joining, you never will be able to join. So if you find a church that is true to the Word of God and the doctrines the Word teaches, unite with it even though you may observe some flaws in the conduct and practice of its members. Do your part to contribute to the spiritual advancement of that church, and your spiritual life will be enriched.

Let me give one word of caution however. It is better not to unite with a church at all than to unite with a modernistic church. By modernistic I mean a church that does not consider the Bible to be the Word of God and does not teach that the death of Christ is essential for salvation. Such churches do not preach the new birth, and they make no effort to win men and women to a personal acceptance of Jesus Christ. In most communities, however, you will usually be able to find a church where you can have true Christian fellowship.

Chapter 12

Your Giving

If you have come to know and love the Lord, naturally it should be one of your desires to do whatever you can to further His work in this world, not only by serving as you can but also by giving of your means to help others serve.

It is tragic that so many Christians use their money selfishly. This is really difficult to understand, because one of the most common demonstrations of love is giving. When you love a person, you instinctively give that person gifts. When a young man starts dating a girl, he begins to buy her candy and flowers and other gifts that he thinks will please her. At Christmastime we give gifts to relatives and friends; we also remember them on their birthdays and anniversaries. Love expresses itself through giving. Because God loved us, He gave us the supreme gift of His only begotten Son.

Of course, people who do not love God will not be interested in giving money to His work, but a person who loves the Lord with all his heart will surely consider it a duty and a privilege to give.

The Bible has much to say about giving. During the Dispensation of the Law, God's people were required to give one-tenth of all their income to the Lord. This tithe, as it was called, was mandatory for all; and in addition to the tithe, they were to add their "gifts."

Christians often ask, "Is tithing a binding law for us now that we are no longer under the Law but under grace?" Although tithing is not a law of the New Testament, the grace of God operating in a believer today cannot expect less of us than what the Law required. Grace should exceed the Law. Many Christians should be ashamed of themselves for giving only a tenth of what they have to the Lord. God has blessed them so abundantly that they should give far more, but they stick to the bare minimum that the Old Testament Law required before the grace of God was fully revealed to mankind.

The rule of grace laid down in the New Testament is to give "as God hath prospered" (I Cor. 16:2). The entire verse reads: "Upon the first day of the week let every one of you lay by him in store, as God hath prospered him, that there be no gatherings when I come." Two general principles are seen in this verse. One is to give regularly: "Upon the first day of the week." The other is to give according to your means: "As God hath prospered." No minimum amount is required in the New Testament, but no maximum limit is established either. Every Christian should give according to what God has entrusted to him.

Another New Testament passage that talks about giving is II Corinthians 9:7: "Every man according as he purposeth in his heart, so let him give; not grudgingly, or of necessity: for God loveth a cheerful giver." The preceding verse says, "But this I say, He which soweth sparingly shall reap also sparingly; and he which soweth bountifully shall reap also bountifully." The Lord Jesus told His disciples, "Give, and it shall be given unto you; good measure, pressed down, and shaken together, and running over, shall men give into your bosom. For with the same measure that ye mete withal it shall be measured to you again" (Luke 6:38).

Giving seems to result in a victorious circle. First, you give as God has prospered you. Then, as you give, God prospers you more so that you can give more. This results in greater prosperity and more giving and so on! Will you put this promise of God and rule of grace to a test? Be a liberal Christian, and God will bless you liberally in return. He always does.

As stated previously, tithing is not a law of the New Testament, but every Christian should have a plan for systematic giving. If you feel honestly before God that He does not expect you to give more than one-tenth of your income, then be very careful to give at least that much to Him. Put His portion aside as soon as you receive your income. Regard that money as no longer yours. If you follow that plan, you will always be giving something to the work of the Lord. Evidently the Apostle Paul saw the value of systematic giving, and for that reason he urged every believer to put aside his offering on the first day of the week. If you take the Lord's portion out of your paycheck or other income first, it will become so habitual that you will never fail to give Him what you should.

But beware of thinking that because you have given a tenth, you have given all that God expects you to. Some Christians could—and should—give half of their income to the Lord. Some could give even more. Remember that God looks not only at what you have given to Him but also at what you have kept for yourself! He knows how much money you need to care for your family properly and to meet your obligations. He knows, too, when you are spending money selfishly and foolishly. Selfishness is the very essence of sin, and you must avoid it. Your one desire in life, both in what you do and in what you earn, should be to glorify the name of Christ and further His work.

Some pastors strongly teach that all the money you give to God must be given to or through your local church. Nothing in Scripture supports this idea. This teaching arises largely from a kind of denominational stinginess. It is usually a mistake to give all of your money to one person or organization. You should spread out your gifts, though not too thinly, so that you may have a share in God's work in various areas. Pastors who encourage giving only to the church claim support for their teaching from Malachi 3:10, which says, "Bring ye all the tithes into the storehouse." They interpret the church as the present-day storehouse. But the church is not like the Old Testament temple. The church has no storehouse and is not a storehouse.

To include the local church in this Old Testament verse seems to be inaccurate Bible interpretation.

You should, of course, give liberally and regularly to your church. But you should also give to other organizations and programs God is using to accomplish His work, such as faith missions and Gospel broadcasts. No Christian has a right to tell another Christian that he should not give his money to these worthy causes. The only time we have the right to advise against giving money to any religious group is when that money will not be used for a Gospel witness or when we know that organization is not true to Christ.

You need to be very careful before giving money to programs outside the church, of course, for some of them are unreliable and unworthy. You should carefully investigate each one. First, make certain that the organization is doctrinally sound. Second, make sure it is financially sound. Any honest religious organization should send numbered receipts for all gifts given. Their accounting records should be audited at least once a year, and the auditors' report should be made available. If you desire to give money to a mission board or to support a missionary with some board, find out if the board is financially responsible. Do they publish regular reports of all monies received? Do they have their records audited by certified public accountants?

Don't give your money to an individual just because you are fascinated by his personality. If you want to give to an individual, make sure he is one of

God's servants and is using the money to spread the Gospel. Never give to increase the wealth of a popular preacher. Give only for the purpose of sharing the Gospel and ministering to a needy world.

Never give your money to modernistic organizations. If you belong to a church whose missionary program is not based on the Word of God, don't give to that program. Instead, find a sound missionary organization you can support. Not all denominational mission boards are modernistic, by any means, but a number of them are. In fact, it was because many of the older boards became modernistic and lost their pioneer spirit that God established independent faith mission boards.

If you have the right attitude toward your redemption, you will have the right attitude toward Christian stewardship. Since you have been redeemed, you belong completely to God. You are not your own, for you have been "bought with a price" (I Cor. 6:20). All that you possess belongs to Him too— your physical strength, your mind, your personality, your possessions and your money. Your money is really God's money. It is only entrusted to you as His steward. If you prove to be a poor steward, He may take it away from you and give it to someone else (see Luke 19:11-26).

You will have to give an account to God, not only for the way you spent your time on earth as a Christian but also for the way you spent your money. If you spend it solely for selfish purposes or for worldly ambitions, you will stand ashamed before your Saviour and will be deprived of the rewards you could have had. Those who give to God's work will share in the rewards just as much as those who actually went to the mission field.

If your husband or wife is not saved, it will be more difficult for you to give to God's work. It is especially difficult for a Christian wife to give if her husband is opposed to it. If you are in that circumstance, ask God to give you wisdom about what you should do.

Even young children who love the Lord should give Him a portion of the money they have, no matter how little it is. Christian parents should teach their children the principles of Christian stewardship. If they learn how to give in childhood, it will be easier for them to give as adults.

Once you begin to give liberally, the blessings God will bring into your life will be one of your greatest joys. Remember, you cannot outgive God! The more you give to Him, the more He will give back to you. And the more He gives back to you, the more you can give to Him again. Join the triumphant Christians who have learned to be faithful stewards of all God has entrusted to them.

Chapter 13

Your Life Companion

One of the most serious decisions every Christian must face is choosing the right husband or wife. No step requires more guidance than this one. It is a tragedy for a Christian young person to marry someone who does not agree with him or her about spiritual things. Examples of this are positively heartbreaking.

It is especially a tragedy when a person who has been called into some kind of Christian service marries a partner who will not go with him or her into that service. What a shame for a person to miss doing God's will because of an unwilling partner! In the Bible we read of Samson. He was a young man of God who missed God's richest blessings and spent the latter part of his life in misery and despair because of uncontrolled affection for the wrong woman.

Wait on God regarding your life partner. Remember Psalm 37:3-5: "Trust in the Lord, and do good. . . . Delight thyself also in the Lord; and he shall give thee the desires of thine heart. Commit thy way unto the Lord; trust also in him; and he shall bring it to pass." This promise, of course, covers many areas of the Christian life, but it is an especially good promise to claim in the matter of choosing your mate. If you trust God and delight to do His will, He will provide the right one for you if it is His will for you to marry.

Do not allow your emotions to cause you to marry a person without praying and waiting on God for guidance. Remember that marriage is to last for a lifetime—until death separates you. Divorce is not the will of God and should never be considered by Christians.

One of my seminary professors, commenting on courtship and marriage, said, "Brethren, there is where you may make or break!" I have never forgotten that. When I think now about my fellow students of those days, I realize that some were made by their marriages while others were broken by theirs.

What kind of person should you marry? Perhaps you have been asking this question. As a Christian, you should not marry a person unless he or she meets certain qualifications. First, he must be a believer. It cannot be the will of God for you to unite with a person who is not a Christian, no matter how much you might feel like doing so. The Bible says, "Be ye not unequally yoked together with unbelievers" (II Cor. 6:14). If you disregard this plain injunction from God, you will later regret it. Do not allow yourself to marry someone who is not saved.

Be firm about this. Make it clear to any person who is apparently in love with you that you will never consider marriage unless you are first united in Christ. You need to be cautious though. Make sure that you do not cause that person to make a false profession of faith simply for the purpose of marrying you. Look for some evidence in the person's life that shows he or she has genuinely trusted Christ as Saviour.

Second, the person you marry must not hinder you from doing whatever work or service God has called you to do. It is tragic for a Christian to be married to someone who refuses to walk on the same path. If a young man who is called to be a pastor marries a young lady who refuses to be a pastor's wife, he is in a sad predicament. If a young woman who is called to the mission field marries a young man who wants to become an American businessman, she will have a sorrowful life. If God has called you to a certain type of work or a definite place of service, remember that He cannot lead you to marry someone who is called to some other kind of work in another place. God is never the author of confusion.

Third, the two of you must agree about major areas of life. While opposites attract, you do not want to marry someone whose likes and dislikes are completely opposite from yours. Consider marriage only to a person with whom you can agree on important matters.

This principle applies in a special way to spiritual matters. Have an understanding about which church you will join after you are married. Nothing is wrong with marrying a person from a denomination different from your own, but decide before marriage which church you will join. You must agree on that or else you will face a constant struggle and your children will suffer.

Ordinarily, the wife should join the church to which her husband belongs. But if he belongs to a modernistic or unspiritual church, the couple should decide together either to join the wife's church or another evangelical church. Be reasonably sure that the two of you agree on major preferences before you join your lives in marriage.

A proper marriage will result from a proper courtship. If the dating period is conducted honorably and prayerfully, it will not terminate in a bad marriage. If godliness is demonstrated by a couple during the time of courtship, there will be little danger of serious problems later. As young people treat each other honorably and ethically and as they pray and seek God's will regarding their future, the Lord will make it clear whether or not they should become husband and wife.

If a young man does not maintain proper morals in a dating relationship, he will undoubtedly show even less after marriage. Christian young women should not allow young men, although they may be professing Christians, to take improper liberties. Young women should be careful about their clothing and posture so that they do not make themselves a temptation to any young man.

Christians who are dating should have prayer together every time they have a date. This should help to keep them pure emotionally and morally.

Sex before marriage is sinful under every circumstance. The Bible consistently terms this "fornication." Indulgence in such relations is not only contrary to the Word of God, but it also destroys the proper affection and respect that should exist between a man and a woman after marriage. No man ever feels quite the same when he marries a woman whose chastity he has already violated. No woman feels the same thrill in marrying a man with whom she has already had marriage relations. Their coming together following the marriage ceremony will never mean the same to either of them. The deep joy of the marriage relationship has been marred and broken.

Nothing is sweeter or purer on this side of heaven than for two Christian young people, of like mind and like calling, to come to the marriage night and give themselves wholly and purely to each other. But nothing is so likely to lead to distrust and bitterness in later life than for either of them to have participated in improper relationships before marriage. Of course, if a man and woman have committed fornication, God does promise forgiveness for those who repent and turn from their sin. But the fact remains that marriage will never mean to either of them what it would have meant if they had remained chaste.

Sometimes young women are overly anxious to be married and allow themselves to be courted and married by the first person who shows them some attention and consideration. But an unmarried woman once said, "I would rather be an old maid than wish I were one!" There is perhaps a touch of humor in that statement but also a great deal of wisdom. If you cannot trust God to bring you a husband, you cannot trust Him to help you live together with a man in a proper relationship after marriage. If God wants you to have a husband, He will bring you one. If it is His will for you to remain single, it certainly would be a tragedy for you to marry. Many mistakes in marriage have been due to haste. People are not willing to wait on God for their life partner. "Wait, I say, on the Lord" (Ps. 27:14).

A happy marriage and home is a foretaste of heaven. An unhappy marriage and home can be a miniature hell.

Chapter 14

Your Family and Home

Once a Christian is married, he must give primary consideration to his home and family. In the Bible, children are regarded as a blessing from the Lord. The psalmist wrote: "Lo, children are an heritage of the Lord. . . . As arrows are in the hand of a mighty man; so are children of the youth. Happy is the man that hath his quiver full of them: they shall not be ashamed" (Ps. 127:3-5).

Raising children is a solemn responsibility, particularly in this age of moral decline. It is the spiritual duty of Christian parents to raise their children "in the nurture and admonition of the Lord" (Eph. 6:4). Discipline will be part of this process. Proverbs 23:13 says, "Withhold not correction from the child: for if thou beatest [punish] him with the rod [switch], he shall not die." The Bible also says, "Chasten thy son while there is hope, and let not thy soul spare for his crying" (Prov. 19:18). While people today consider instructions such as these to be old-fashioned and outdated, they are commands included in the Word of God and they contain proven principles.

Above all, Christian parents are to teach their

108

children the Scriptures and the knowledge of God. Through Moses, God commanded, "These words, which I command thee this day, shall be in thine heart: and thou shalt teach them diligently unto thy children, and shalt talk of them when thou sittest in thine house" (Deut. 6:6,7). Any parent is too busy who cannot take the time to read the Bible to the children and to teach them the story of Jesus and the meaning of prayer. Faithfully teaching your children must be your highest priority as a parent. It is the supreme privilege and the solemn obligation of Christian parents to point their children to the Saviour, Jesus Christ, and to the way of salvation through Him.

As a parent, you must spend time with your children. You can have no greater influence on your children than by spending time with them. Talk with them. Play with them. Take walks with them. Answer all of their childish questions as best you can. Never ignore your child's questions, no matter how simple or profound. Never give the child a response of indifference or avoidance. Small children idolize their parents; they believe that you know everything and can do anything.

One of the greatest needs children have is to know that their parents love them. Do not disillusion them about this. To cause a child to doubt his parents' love and care for him is to deal that child a psychological blow from which he may never recover. Every Christian parent should continually reassure his children of his love and affection and demonstrate that love in his life.

109

Exercise patience in dealing with your children. They are well worth the investment! Discipline them, when they need it, in patience and love. Never punish them in anger or in a fit of temper. When children are reproved and punished in a concerned and reasonable way, they will not only receive it but also will eventually thank you for it.

In our day it is often necessary for the wife to work outside the home. But even though this may be necessary, her first place of responsibility is to her family in the home. When both parents work, children are often turned over to baby-sitters or child care services. Even if such services are staffed by Christians, they cannot adequately provide the spiritual training children should receive from their mothers. No one can take the place of a parent's presence, love and discipline. If the vital ingredient of parental companionship is omitted from a child's early life, that loss may take a bitter toll in later years. Many parents might have avoided hours of grief if they had invested a little more time and love in the lives of their children in their early years. Christian parents especially must take time to do this. It is a God-given duty and an indispensable part of wise and good parenthood.

Parental responsibility also demands taking the time to counsel children regarding moral and social integrity. Children must be warned of the problems they will face throughout life, and none can do this better than their Christian parents. Good parents must counsel their children about how to avoid the social and moral traps of life. They must teach their children, both by word and by example, how to live pure, upright and faithful lives—before others and before God.

The right conjugal relationship between husband and wife is essential to a real Christian home. The Bible gives wise and practical counsel to husbands about this: "Let thy fountain be blessed: and rejoice with the wife of thy youth" (Prov. 5:18). "Husbands, love your wives, even as Christ also loved the church, and gave himself for it" (Eph. 5:25). "Ye husbands, dwell with them according to knowledge, giving honour unto the wife, . . . that your prayers be not hindered" (I Pet. 3:7).

Concerning the wives, the Bible says, "Teach the young women to be sober, to love their husbands, to love their children" (Titus 2:4). "Wives, submit yourselves unto your own husbands, as unto the Lord" (Eph. 5:22). "Ye wives, be in subjection to your own husbands; that, if any obey not the word, they also may without the word be won by the conversation [behavior] of the wives" (I Pet. 3:1).

Marriage vows are intended to last for life—"until death do us part." Many forget this. Divorce has now become a way of life, even in so-called Christian countries. But God never sanctioned divorce. He only tolerates it because of human perversity. In the New Testament, we are told that the Pharisees came to Jesus "tempting him, and saying unto him, Is it lawful for a man to put away his wife for every cause? And he answered and said unto them, Have ye not read, that he which made them at the beginning made them male and female, and said, For this

111

cause shall a man leave father and mother, and shall cleave to his wife: and they twain shall be one flesh? . . . What therefore God hath joined together, let not man put asunder. They say unto him, Why did Moses then command to give a writing of divorcement, and to put her away? He saith unto them, Moses because of the hardness of your hearts suffered you to put away your wives: but from the beginning it was not so. And I say unto you, Whosoever shall put away his wife, except it be for fornication, and shall marry another, committeth adultery" (Matt. 19:3-9).

The Apostle Paul, under the inspiration of the Holy Spirit, wrote: "Unto the married I command, yet not I, but the Lord, Let not the wife depart from her husband: but and if she depart, let her remain unmarried, or be reconciled to her husband: and let not the husband put away his wife. . . . If any brother hath a wife that believeth not, and she be pleased to dwell with him, let him not put her away. And the woman which hath an husband that believeth not, and if he be pleased to dwell with her, let her not leave him. For the unbelieving husband is sanctified by the wife, and the unbelieving wife is sanctified by the husband" (I Cor. 7:10-14). In the same passage he says, "But if the unbelieving depart, let him depart. A brother or a sister is not under bondage in such cases" (v. 15).

The question is often asked, "What about the person who has been divorced and remarried but now wants to live for God? Should he go on living with the one to whom he is presently married or be separated from that mate?" In dealing with this matter, Paul said, "Let every man abide in the same calling wherein he was called" (I Cor. 7:20). He later repeats that statement, undoubtedly for emphasis and clarity: "Brethren, let every man, wherein he is called, therein abide with God" (v. 24). Paul realized that two wrongs do not make a right and that anyone who surrenders himself or herself to Christ should remain in the civil status he or she was in at the time of that surrender.

The Bible is clear that no Christian has the right to divorce his mate, except for adultery. In cases where there has been divorce and remarriage, obviously the right thing to do is to live in a proper relationship with the current partner in the fear of the Lord and with a true desire to please Him. The Bible makes it plain that divorce is wrong and displeasing to God. But this sin, like any other, can be forgiven.

Chapter 15

Pitfalls to Avoid

In closing this book, I wish to point out some problems to be avoided as you seek to walk with Christ. You will stumble at times along the way. No one has ever yet walked perfectly from the time of his salvation until he went home to meet the Lord. So when you stumble, don't allow Satan to discourage you or keep you down. Get up, confess your sins, ask for new grace and go on! Like Paul, you should "press toward the mark for the prize of the high calling of God in Christ Jesus" (Phil. 3:14).

First, do not focus on others. The psalmist said, "It is better to trust in the Lord than to put confidence in man" (Ps. 118:8). Many young Christians have become discouraged because they followed too closely some other Christian whom they considered to be almost perfect. Then when that Christian failed, they could not understand it. It is good to look up to other Christians, particularly older and more mature Christians, and to receive help from them, but always remember that even the best Christian is only a human being and he may bitterly disappoint you.

It is a serious blow when someone you have

looked up to, possibly even a pastor, falls into sin. But if you have your eyes on Jesus instead of on a human being, your faith will not be destroyed even though you may be disappointed and saddened. The writer to the Hebrews said we should "run with patience the race that is set before us, looking unto Jesus the author and finisher of our faith" (Heb. 12:1,2). Some people are converted to a person instead of to Christ. They are candidates for disappointment. But as long as you keep your eyes on Jesus Christ, you will never be disappointed.

Second, do not place too much importance on material goods. Paul, writing to young Timothy, warned, "They that will be rich fall into temptation and a snare, and into many foolish and hurtful lusts. . . . For the love of money is the root of all evil" (I Tim. 6:9,10). Throughout Scripture the danger of wealth and material prosperity is emphasized, and Jesus spoke of the difficulty a rich man would have in entering the kingdom of heaven. In explaining His parable about the seed and the sower to His disciples, He said, "The cares of this world, and the deceitfulness of riches, and the lusts of other things entering in, choke the word, and it becometh unfruitful" (Mark 4:19). Material riches are indeed deceitful. The more possessions you accumulate, the more time you want to spend in acquiring still more.

Some Christians have been so preoccupied with materialism that they have neglected prayer, Bible reading, church attendance, evangelism and every other spiritual activity. They claim to be busy "looking after their job." But behind what appears to be an innocent and honorable goal is an insatiable desire to accumulate the wealth of this world at any cost. The Lord Jesus also said, "Lay not up for yourselves treasures upon earth, where moth and rust doth corrupt, and where thieves break through and steal: but lay up for yourselves treasures in heaven" (Matt. 6:19,20).

Whenever you sense that you are giving in to the temptation of materialism, go to God in prayer and ask Him for victory over your desires. Have only one objective for everything you possess—to use it for Christ's glory, making sure that you are also providing adequately for normal living expenses and the care of your family.

Third, do not become too friendly with those who would hinder your spiritual growth. It was emphasized in an earlier chapter that believers should not encourage intimate relationships with unspiritual people. Such people, even though they may be professing Christians, can drag you down spiritually and lead you away from close fellowship with God. Whenever you feel a person's influence is leading you away from Christ, make your association with that person less intimate.

Fourth, do not participate in gossip or criticism. Many Christians have ruined their spiritual lives by becoming critical and bitter. It is easy to criticize another or to spread gossip, yet it is detrimental to your own spiritual welfare. A minister of the Gospel once said to me, "When I feel myself becoming critical, I just take a good, square look at Jesus!"

Fifth, beware of pride, conceit and self-confidence. Some statements from Scripture explain this warning. "For I say, through the grace given unto me, to every man that is among you, not to think of himself more highly than he ought to think" (Rom. 12:3). "Humble yourselves in the sight of the Lord, and he shall lift you up" (James 4:10). "Pride goeth before destruction, and an haughty spirit before a fall" (Prov. 16:18). "An high look, and a proud heart, and the plowing of the wicked, is sin" (21:4). "Let him that thinketh he standeth take heed lest he fall" (I Cor. 10:12). "God resisteth the proud, but giveth grace unto the humble. Submit yourselves therefore to God" (James 4:6,7).

Here is a final word of exhortation and encouragement: "Therefore, my beloved brethren, be ye stedfast, unmoveable, always abounding in the work of the Lord, forasmuch as ye know that your labour is not in vain in the Lord" (I Cor. 15:58).

Back to the Bible is a nonprofit ministry dedicated to Bible teaching, evangelism and edification of Christians worldwide.

If we may assist you in knowing more about Christ and the Christian life, please write to us without obligation:

Back to the Bible
P.O. Box 82808
Lincoln, NE 68501